D0310739

HERCULES THE BEAR

MAGGIE ROBIN

HERCULES THE BEAR

A GENTLE GIANT IN THE FAMILY

THE MOVING BIOGRAPHY OF THE 'UNTAMEABLE' GRIZZLY BEAR WHO BECAME A NATIONAL HERO

metro

Published in Great Britain by Metro Publishing,
an imprint of
John Blake Publishing Limited
3 Bramber Court, 2 Bramber Road
London W14 9PB

www.johnblakepublishing.co.uk

www.facebook.com/johnblakebooks ▪
twitter.com/jblakebooks ▪

First published in hardback in 2001 by Noel Collins Ltd, Edinburgh
Revised, expanded and updated edition first published in hardback
in 2015 by Metro Publishing

ISBN: 978-1-78418-815-3

British Library Cataloguing-in-Publication Data:

A catalogue record for this book is available from the British Library.

Design by www.envydesign.co.uk

Printed in Great Britain by CPI Group (UK) Ltd

1 3 5 7 9 10 8 6 4 2

Papers used by John Blake Publishing are natural, recyclable products made from
wood grown in sustainable forests. The manufacturing processes conform to the
environmental regulations of the country of origin.

Every attempt has been made to contact the relevant copyright-holders, but some
were unobtainable. We would be grateful if the appropriate people could contact us.

CONTENTS

This book is dedicated with affection and gratitude to the Islanders of Benbecula, and in memory of Mum and Dad; also in memory of our good friend Eddie Orbell, without whom this amazing adventure would not have been possible.

ACKNOWLEDGEMENTS

Throughout our life with Hercules we have been fortunate to have been involved with some very special people. I would like to acknowledge them for their kindness, wisdom, help and friendship.

Firstly, David Summnall of Middlechild Productions, with whom we entrusted Hercules's story – thank you David.

My mum, dad and family, especially my sister Hazel and her family, who are always there for us.

My cousin John Maclean of North Uist and his family, who helped us enormously with the moving of Hercules to his final resting place.

My relatives and the islanders of Grimsay and North Uist for their friendship and support.

Roger Wheater, the former Director of Edinburgh Zoo.

Numerous friends and neighbours who took to living with a bear as the most natural thing in the world.

Our dear friend the late Sir Hugh Fraser for his boundless enthusiastic support.

The late Eddie Orbell of the Highland Wildlife Park, a man full of kindness and an immense love of animals.

Hercules's fans and admirers who touched our subconscious mind and taught us to appreciate our fellow man.

Anne Logan, our kindest caring vet, who helped us through.

My heroes, local farmers David Johnman and Jimmy Patterson, always ready to help.

Martin Palmer and Toby Buchan at John Blake Publishing for believing in our story.

And finally, the British media, who treated Hercules and ourselves with respect.

MAGGIE ROBIN

CHAPTER 1

GRIZZLY BEAR

Hercules lay sleeping as I wrote part of this with his head on my feet. Earlier he had been playing with the cushion which was peeping out from under his enormous bottom, occasionally tossing it into the air and catching it in his paws. I told him, 'Uh-uh, not the cushion,' and he looked at me as if to say, 'Come on, Mum, what do you take me for?', tucked it under his tummy and settled down to watch television.

It was a raw afternoon in November when I first started to write my book. The icy rain was coming down the Glen in great swaths of grey, battering against the old house. Andy had gone out to chop wood for the fire. He cut his logs a metre long and we put them straight into the enormous hearth blazing beside me. On days like that, when the fire was stacked high, it was useful to have someone like Hercules around to help me lift them.

The room, our sitting room, was probably very like your sitting room, with armchairs and sofa, TV and photos on the walls – an ordinary-sized room with ordinary objects. The house it was in, our home at that time, was the Sheriffmuir Inn, off a narrow back road that led to the A9, the main road to the north of Scotland. The Parish of Sheriffmuir – there isn't really a village – is between Stirling and Dunblane.

When I looked out of the window here on a fine day there was no sign of humankind. The Ochil Mountains rose around us – a vanguard of the great mountains that form the centre of Scotland. We were on the edge of the old Highland Line, and the people round here would have spoken Gaelic in the old days. Further down the Glen the land was cultivated in small fields and there were plantations of pine trees. In front of the Inn, and on the other side of the road there was a fast-flowing burn, fed from the mountains, in which Andy and Hercules loved to play in the warm weather.

The house was over three hundred years old. It was here that the famous Battle of Sheriffmuir was fought on a misty November day in 1715; indeed, the Inn was used as the headquarters of the Earl of Mar, who led the Jacobite army. Mar and his Highlanders were trying to break through to join the Jacobites who had risen in the northwest of England, when they met the Duke of Argyll at the head of a disciplined army of Hanoverian troops. They fought all day in the mist and the Clan Macrae were slaughtered to a man. In the end there was no conclusive victor. Sometimes, on dark days, one can almost imagine the kilted clansmen moving down the hillsides with gory broadswords in their hands . . . If stones could speak the old Inn would have some strange tales to tell, but perhaps none stranger than the story I love to tell about the battle of wits between a man and a grizzly bear.

As I relaxed in front of the fire my thoughts drifted back to the day a young man, a stranger to us, came to the Inn to see for himself this bear called 'Hercules' that he had heard so much about. He had spent many years in the north of Canada and in the Arctic, and had seen bears in the wild – both grizzlies and their near cousin the polar bear.

Andy noted his enthusiastic interest and took him to meet Herc in his den, which he refused to come into and instead stood at the door incredulously repeating, 'I don't believe it; this can't be real; I must be dreaming,' while Herc kissed and cuddled his dad.

Years ago, he told us, when he was working in the north of Canada, he had joined the search party for a friend who had gone off alone on a fishing expedition. They found his tent and there were bears' footprints in the snow all round it. In an instant they knew that their worst fears had been confirmed and he prayed that his friend had been knocked senseless by the first blow from the huge hungry creature that had found the camp. He refused to go to the actual spot where his friend had obviously ended his days. All that was found of him was some shreds of clothing, a belt buckle and his false teeth.

On another occasion, further north, he had watched a polar bear sitting over a hole in the ice, patiently waiting for a seal to pop up. After a while a large seal weighing about

200 pounds duly appeared and slithered into the frozen air. With one movement the bear was on it, and with another he had delivered a massive swipe with his front paw that lifted the broken seal into the air and flung it like a toy over the ice. When the bear had moved off, he crept down and measured just how far the seal had been flung by that one blow: it was 66 feet.

I could well believe it. When Hercules was younger there was a tree trunk in his den. It was about 4 feet long and about 4 feet in diameter. It was oak, and so heavy that even Andy couldn't lift it and had to rock it from side to side to move it about the den. Hercules would pat it from paw to paw, sliding it easily across the floor, like a child with a toy. Once, when he was in a particularly mischievous mood, he picked up the log and used it as a battering ram to knock down a wall.

In Yellowstone | National Park, in the USA, a grizzly once killed a large black bear with a single swipe. The punch was so strong that it knocked the black bear against a tree 16 feet away.

At my feet Hercules stirred in his sleep and stretched out a front paw. My old *Chambers's Encyclopaedia* solemnly says of the great cuddly heap at my feet, 'No animal in the New World is more formidable.' Native Americans believed that he was created to be more powerful and more clever than all other creatures: once he was created, runs the legend, even the god who made him, Manitou, had to flee to the top of a mountain to escape him. He would have had to flee fast, what is more, for over a distance of up to 150 metres a grizzly bear can run as fast as a good horse.

In spite of their fearful reputation – 'more fierce and carnivorous than any other bear except the polar bear', says the encyclopedia – and in spite of the numerous exaggerated stories of the Old West in which bands of grizzlies attack homesteads during hard winters, bears are in fact timid creatures.

One experienced bear hunter of a hundred years ago remarked in his memoirs, 'I have pursued a great many bears and every one of them fled before me; not a single one showed any intention of defending itself.' Only when they are surprised are they likely to attack, particularly when there are cubs or if they are disturbed when hibernating, and this they do by rearing on their hind legs, swinging their front paws and growling. Most experts agree that this posture is basically a display, meant only to intimidate the foe, and certainly a bear usually knocks its opponent down with a swipe and then moves away.

If they are attacked, of course, bears will attempt to defend themselves, and there are numerous stories – again from the Old West – of bear hunters being chased. In 1805, the great American explorer Meriwether Lewis was chased for 100 metres by a badly wounded bear and, two days later, this unfortunate animal was shot eight times with a rifle and still kept coming at them.

Today, in parts of Canada and the United States where there are still plenty of bears, they are viewed with awe and respect, and not a little fear. I spoke to someone recently who had asked an old-timer backwoodsman what he should do if he met a bear. The old fellow sucked on his pipe and said with deliberation that the first thing to do was to climb a tree, then it depended on whether the bear was a black bear or a grizzly. 'How will I be able to tell?' asked my friend. The old timer replied, 'Wal, if it's one of them there black beyers he'll jist come up th' tree after you; but, if it's a grizzly, why, he'll jist knock that ole tree down!'

People walking in the national parks where bears are to be found wear 'bear bells' round their necks to warn of their approach and avoid the possibility of surprising any bears. But accidents occur. Funnily enough, bears who live close to humans, and rely on scraps and garbage left behind by picnickers for the main part of their diet, become even more dangerous, and there are always stories of picnickers being eaten up by a bear, though it happens very rarely.

Andy and I were always conscious of the risk attached even to the great big softie snoring away in front of the fire. But we knew him very, very well now, and we believed it would take a brain injury or something equally serious to make him run amok.

Mind you, every time I heard horrendous bear stories, it did make me pause for thought, but not for long – like the story early in our relationship of a black bear called Smokey. That bear was normally chained up and muzzled and used to wrestle his owner. The wrestler's girlfriend never had any contact with that bear and was never allowed to touch him. She was blonde, like me, and the same age . . .

Usually after an 'accident' like that the bear is shot, though in this case the Canadian Government took the bear into care – thankfully. Andy and I made sure that we left a document with our lawyers stating that, should anything happen to us, no matter what, Hercules was not to be blamed or harmed.

Herc growled in his sleep, probably dreaming about his terrible ordeal in the wild when he was lost in the Outer Hebrides. I will tell you all about this in its place. First of all, I must tell you how a man won the love and trust of a grizzly bear, something the whole world said was impossible, and, in order to do that I must introduce you to my husband, 'Grizzly' Andy Robin.

CHAPTER 2

GRIZZLY
ANDY ROBIN

Little did I know as I was getting my horses ready to go to the Perth Agricultural Show on that hot August morning in 1972 that the day would prove to be one of the great turning points in my life. As I busied myself in the stables making sure that my horses were groomed and that the horsebox was prepared, I had no thoughts about the day other than that I hoped to do well in the events for which I was entered and that I might meet a few friends there.

As a farmer's daughter I was well used to going to agricultural shows, which were always full of ruddy-faced farmers dressed in their best tweed suits with their endless talk of barley and wheat, topsoil and seed potatoes. For some people they aren't the most exciting places in the world, but

I always longed for them, as they gave me an opportunity to ride in competition.

I had never been to the Perth Show before, as I had preferred, until then, to compete in the more local shows that took place on the same day. A simple twist of fate made me decide to go to Perth that day, and how glad I was in the coming years that fate had made me do so.

I arrived at the show a short while before my first event was due to begin; and, having tacked up the horses and collected my numbers from the show secretary, I had plenty of time to wander around the stalls.

As I strolled from the newly mown ring back to my horsebox I was suddenly aware that I was being stared at. Turning round to get a better look, I found myself facing a large suntanned man with the most piercing blue eyes I had ever seen. He was not so much tall as big, and, to my consternation, he was smiling at me, although I knew I had never set eyes on him before. I began to blush and dropped my head quickly to avoid his stare, which seemed to be saying, 'You don't know me yet, but you will.'

I hurriedly made for my horsebox and began busying myself with the final preparations. As I struggled with saddles and bridles, I put the brief episode out of my mind and by the time I had changed into my breeches and navy jacket I had forgotten all about him.

However, as I was warming up in the collecting area outside the show ring I noticed that the suntanned gentleman was once again standing behind me and, trying to ignore him, I went about the business of limbering up each horse, taking them in turn over the red and white fence that stood in the middle of the practice area. I could not help glancing in his direction and, each time I did so, I was met by the same penetrating stare and wry smile, and, each time, I felt myself turning crimson with embarrassment.

Luck was not with me that day and, although I managed one clear round, I finished the event with a miserable fifth place. Feeling suitably humbled, I made my way back to the horsebox to wipe down the horses and put on their travelling bandages.

I was stabling that night with Mr and Mrs Drummond, local farmers at Forteviot, who were directors of the show, and, as they were not yet ready to leave, I had time to kill. As I sat and watched the other competitors leading horses back to horseboxes I saw a crowd beginning to gather round a smaller ring that had been hastily erected in the centre of the arena. I decided to investigate, and made my way into the thick of the crowd.

I managed to find a place for myself at the front of what was clearly a wrestling or boxing ring just as two burly figures stepped into it. At that moment I noticed that the man who had stared at me earlier was standing just in front of me, but now he was wearing a pair of blue trunks and had a tartan towel slung casually over his huge muscular shoulders. It was now obvious that he was at the show to wrestle, and seemed to be a popular figure, judging by the number of backslapping farmers who surrounded him.

I fidgeted self-consciously trying to appear nonchalant as he moved towards me. As the bout started he drew me into a one-sided conversation, explaining holds and throws, pins and falls, such information being deftly interwoven with a smooth chat-up routine.

He was next on the bill and I was slightly shocked to see someone who had been talking to me in a relaxed way suddenly change into a grunting heaving brute as he mercilessly pummelled his opponent; and yet I had to admire the ease and efficiency of every superbly executed movement, which quickly led to the submission of his foe.

After the bout, I left the showground, wondering at and intrigued by the roughness of my new acquaintance, who had been led triumphantly from the ring while his opponent had been carried off on a stretcher. I wondered if our paths would ever cross again, but doubted they would, which was probably a good thing, as I knew he was not the sort of man my mother would want me to bring home for tea.

How wrong could I be? The very next day the persistent stranger rang my home, though it is anyone's guess how he got my number, and after much persuasion I reluctantly agreed to go out with him.

As the weeks passed, we began to see more and more of each other, and for the first time in my life I found myself becoming deeply interested in something other than my horses. Andy could not have been further removed from the boy next door, but as we got to know each other we discovered that we both had a deep love of animals and the outdoor life. At first my parents, while not openly saying so, made it clear that they did not approve of my association with Andy. Like all parents, they wanted the best for their children and expected me to settle down and marry a kind, honest farming man like my father. They had heard stories from their friends that Andy was a ladies' man with a chequered past, a disreputable job and an insecure future.

In time when they realised that trying to dissuade me from seeing him was useless and they came to know him better from his frequent visits to our house, they began to grow fond of him despite their preconceived ideas.

Gradually, Andy began to win my parents' respect with his infectious enthusiasm and his determination to get on in life. He had to be determined, because he began life in Stirling, the son of a hardworking miner, in a community where there was no real alternative to the pit, and sons followed fathers in going down it. It was a life of unremitting toil and considerable hardship, and, seeing his father's life and what prospects lay before him, Andy swore at an early age that he would do everything in his power to avoid going down the mine, and vowed to work in the open air.

As a child Andy loved being outdoors and developed a love for animals that kept him constantly in trouble. His parents had to watch every penny carefully and they could not afford to keep a pet, nor was there room for one in their tiny house.

This did not deter Andy, who would befriend any animal he met and bring it back into the house. Time and again the family's evening meal would be interrupted by an indignant neighbour banging on the door asking if Andy had 'borrowed' their dog, and, sure enough, the animal would be found hidden in Andy's bedroom. It was not just the usual domestic pets that caught Andy's fancy: he would also smuggle in owls and rabbits that he found when roaming in the countryside.

When Andy was twelve he found a stray spaniel. For once, he tried to find out who the owner of the dog was, but none could be found, and so he kept the dog – which he called Sammy – hidden in a shed and fed him on titbits taken secretly from the larder. Sammy was a natural retriever and would bring back anything that Andy threw for him, picking up the object in his soft mouth and laying it at Andy's feet. One day Andy took Sammy for a walk in the countryside near his home, and on the way they took a shortcut through a nearby farmyard. In the farmyard were a number of ducks, and Andy had considerable trouble stopping the over-eager spaniel from picking up the ducklings that were waddling around the yard.

The next day, when Andy came back from school, he discovered two ducklings in the shed and no Sammy. He hurriedly put the ducklings into a sack and went off to deliver them back to the farm. When he got back home he found Sammy in the shed with another duckling, and this time when he went back to the farm he ran into the furious farmer, who was convinced that Andy had been stealing his ducks. Poor Andy was in trouble again!

His first job was on a farm and his mother personally delivered him to the farmer in the hope that some hard outdoor work would begin to channel his limitless energies in the right direction. But this was not to be, for he felt terribly hemmed in by the routine work on the farm, and one night he sneaked out of his bothy and ran away.

It was soon after leaving the farm that Andy at last found something he really liked doing, when he was given the opportunity to start in the timber business. The work was entirely outdoors and intensely physical; Andy thrived on it. In time, by working all the hours God gave him, he managed to save enough money to go into business on his own.

Going into business on his own meant just what it says and, equipped with only a saw and a horse and cart, Andy would single-handedly fell the timber, load it, transport it and unload it. His capacity for hard work quickly earned him the nickname 'the Beast' in the timber trade, for he became immensely strong.

One day after Andy had cut down a tree he noticed that a jackdaws' nest was lodged in the fallen branches. There were two fledglings in the nest, who had obviously been abandoned by their mother when the tree was felled. Andy's big soft heart couldn't let him leave the two helpless birds and so 'the Beast' adopted them. He called the two birds Jackie and Mary and raised them in his house. When the birds were fully fledged he released them but they would always come to be fed, and it was not uncommon for Andy to be seen with a jackdaw perched on each shoulder. When he was working they would sit easily, relaxing on the head of his giant Alsatian, Rex. Sadly, one day as Andy was coming out of his timber store, the birds flew to meet him and, not knowing they were behind the door, Andy opened it and crushed poor Jackie. Mary was heartbroken and within a short time she pined to death.

Not content with running himself into the ground at

work every day, Andy became involved in amateur boxing, but, when he saw the damage the sport inflicted on the faces of the young boxers, coupled with the fact that he was being continually reprimanded by referees for grappling with his opponents, he decided boxing was not for him, and he turned his attentions to wrestling instead.

Discovering that he had a natural flair for the sport, Andy took up wrestling seriously and started his career by attending the numerous Highland games meetings that took place each summer, all over Scotland. At one of the meetings he met a fellow wrestler called Willie Bell and they decided to go into partnership. The pair soon established themselves on the circuit and were among the most successful competitors in Scotland.

Success followed success for the persistent Scot and, while only twenty, he won the World Cumberland Wrestling Championship. Having won the championship he was asked to go to Canada to take part in a festival of sport called 'The Wonderful World of Sport', joining a select group of Scottish athletes who were going to demonstrate Scottish sports such as tossing the caber and throwing the hammer.

He set off for Canada in a second-hand kilt with a breadknife stuck down his sock in place of a skean dhu! The show played to full houses throughout Canada and America and Andy grew more and more confident in his own abilities as a wrestler, and more professional in his handling of audiences.

However, fate had decided that Andy was not to complete the tour. When the show reached Toronto it was discovered that there had been a mistake in the bookings at the Maple Leaf Gardens and, instead of being on the Thursday, as they thought, the show was not to take place until the following night. The Thursday evening booking was a professional wrestling spectacular, and Andy, with lots of free time on his hands, hung around the stadium while the auditorium staff prepared the ring. As he was about to leave he was approached by the promoter, Frank Tunney, who said that one of the wrestlers booked to appear that night had been injured in a fight on the previous evening and, as they were desperately in need of a replacement, would Andy have a go?

Eager for the extra cash it would provide, he accepted and made his way back to the digs to get his kit together.

It was with some trepidation that he entered the floodlit ring that night for his first major professional bout. But his nervousness was calmed as he heard the crowd, many of whom were Scottish Canadians, roaring their support when they saw he was wearing the kilt.

Andy won the bout and when he returned to his dressing room he was met again by Frank Tunney, who offered him a two-year contract to wrestle all over Canada and the US. Always ready for adventure, Andy quickly signed the contract and over those two years he refined and polished his wrestling skills. His professional career was by now fully established and, just when he should have been consolidating his position, he agreed to take on the most hazardous bout of his life. He was booked to fight Terrible Ted.

Terrible Ted was no normal wrestler: he was a black bear.

At the time of agreeing to fight, Andy was not aware of this, but, when told, he agreed nevertheless. The bear would be chained and muzzled, and, if Andy could hold his own, he was guaranteed a thousand dollars in prize money.

The arena was packed that night, and the air heavy with anticipation. As Andy walked down the aisle and waved to the cheering crowd he became increasingly aware of just what he was letting himself in for. If Ted were to get a good grip he could easily crush the life out of him and it wouldn't matter one bit whether the bear was muzzled or not.

Ted stood in the middle of the ring, towering above Andy, making strange growling noises through his shiny black muzzle, and Andy swears to this day that, if he hadn't been wearing the kilt and hadn't felt that he would be letting Scotland down if he didn't go through with it, he would have turned and fled.

Suddenly, a thousand dollars seemed a paltry sum to be paid for risking one's life, and, as he dodged the massive swipes of Ted's front paws and manoeuvred himself out of corners where he might be trapped within the huge bear's grasp, Andy not only felt genuinely more threatened than he had ever been before, but he also recognised the enormous spirit of the magnificent creature.

In the following days he kept reliving the fight with Terrible Ted, which had been so unlike fighting another man and yet strangely similar. In those few minutes an uncanny understanding had grown up between the bear and himself – an understanding hampered only by the fact that Ted was kept constantly chained and muzzled. 'What sort of relationship could develop,' thought Andy, 'between a man and a bear if that bear was treated, without fear, as a genuine equal?' From that moment onwards Andy determined that he would one day find out.

CHAPTER 3

THE IMPOSSIBLE DREAM

Long before we were married, Andy and I agreed that we would do everything we could to share our lives with a wrestling bear. This was to be no ordinary wrestling bear, however, chained and trained only to entertain, degraded into a dangerous clown. That was not the idea. Andy had a vision of an animal that would spar with him on equal terms, a friend and companion whose dignity and independence would be recognised, and who would show the world that trust and companionship were the only ways to achieve results; a wrestling bear who would discredit for ever the tradition of bearbaiting and wrestling with mutilated animals.

We knew that the chances were slender, and the responsibility enormous. A bear can live for up to forty years and cost a fortune to feed. Our whole lives would have to be devoted to him.

Bears were so much a part of Andy that it never occurred to me to question his obsession. I met my first bear in the bear park on Loch Lomondside, where we were enquiring about cubs. An enormous she-bear with two little teddy bear cubs crossed the road in front of our car. She came round and glared menacingly through the car window, which was mercifully closed, and then went on her way. I was very afraid, but nevertheless, from that moment, I was infected by Andy's enthusiasm.

Finding a bear to own was a different thing altogether. Some zoos adopted an incredulous and snooty attitude towards us: they agreed it was preposterous to suppose that such unpredictable and extremely dangerous animals could be made 'pets' of, and they were not prepared to sell a bear into the barbaric slavery of chained performance. We thought at the time, 'What difference is there between chained performance and close imprisonment?' and tried elsewhere.

Then, in December 1974, we heard that a she-bear in the Highland Wildlife Park at Kincraig was pregnant. We contacted Eddie Orbell the director, and after meeting us he said he was prepared to sell us a cub for £50, but he insisted that the cub remain with its mother until it was weaned. He didn't expect that we would keep the cub for more than a week. At this time Mary, the she-bear, had not yet given birth.

There were three cubs in her litter, christened by Andy:

Atlas, Hercules and Samson. Atlas was the largest, and Samson the smallest. They seemed more adventurous than Hercules, rolling about and playing with one another, while Hercules stayed close to his mother. We saw them first in February 1975, and were captivated by their antics, especially by little Hercules. He was already standing unsteadily on his hind legs like a little furry man and had a ring of white baby fur round his stumpy neck.

We left him to suckle under the expert and gentle care of Eddie and said that we would be back as often as we could to keep up with his changes. Over the next seven months we travelled to Kincraig many times, watching him grow in leaps and bounds, until the great day came when he would be ours.

We had borrowed a crate from Edinburgh Zoo and travelled up in our Volkswagen caravanette, towing our horse trailer to enable us to spend the night in the park and leave in plenty of time for moving Hercules the next morning. That evening we drank mugs of cocoa and went over our plans with Eddie and his wife, Joanne. Although we couldn't persuade them that we would achieve our dream, at least Eddie could see that we would take great care of his precious baby. This in some measure allayed his doubts about letting us have Hercules in the first place.

We were up with the birds next morning, impatient to get on with the difficult task of moving Hercules away from his mum and into the horsebox. He was ten months old and weighed 13 stone. Even at this age he was stronger than the average man. It was necessary to tranquillise him before moving him. Eddie gave him the shot while we all kept clear of his sharp teeth.

Even as he went under, his little lip curled in a half-hearted snarl of defiance, but by the time he came round we were ready to go. Farewells were said and everyone agreed that they expected to see Hercules back within the month, but all were very interested to hear what the outcome of our adventure would be. We backed the trailer carefully down the cinder track and were off on the open highway to Sheriffmuir, stopping after an hour or so to make sure our precious cargo was safe, and have a bite of breakfast in a Little Chef restaurant.

Over the blue Formica table we wondered nervously how long Hercules would take to adapt. Would the movement of the horsebox throw him into a rage? Andy had saved a piece of his roll and spread it with tomato ketchup as a treat for our new baby. He took it gently and his little sleepy eyes lit up as he licked off the sweet sauce.

We had built a spacious den for Hercules behind the Inn, very close to the back door. It was made of white-emulsioned stone and connected to an area almost as big as the house itself, which was securely surrounded by a high fence of iron bars. In the den were a couple of rubber tyres, a tree trunk and various other toys for our new baby, and beside it was a hayshed.

Our first task was to move Hercules from his crate into his new home, and this time it would be without any tranquilliser, so you can imagine the tingling nervousness we felt as we realised that anything could happen. Gently, we backed the trailer up to the small door of the den, leaving just enough room to drop the ramp, and slid the heavy crate into the entrance. By this time Hercules was slowly and deliberately weighing the situation up as he stood on all fours, fully awake and ready for action.

As we opened the sliding door of the crate he took off at a rate of knots, panic-stricken, but thinking clearly enough to try to establish the best way out – and hopefully away from these strange new people who now had such a say in his life. Within seconds, he disappeared into his sleeping quarters, noticed immediately a gap between the top of the wall and the hayshed and frantically tried to climb up to it. He seemed to spot every potential escape route within seconds, his eyes darting this way and that and missing nothing. His instinct for survival had put him on the defence right away.

After about fifteen minutes he began to settle down and wandered from one part of his den to the other, sniffing at corners and handles. We watched him silently, and then, out of the blue, Andy announced that, if they were to begin getting to know each other, there was no time like the present to start. We were still the enemy, but what would young Hercules's reaction be if the hand of friendship were offered?

It didn't take long to find out. Armed with a large carton of strawberry ice cream Andy entered the outside run. The cuddly little bear wore an expression of deep suspicion as he stood his ground, eyes wide with fear. Both parties then remained perfectly still, each leaving it to the other to make the first move. After some time the little black button of a snout sniffed the air in the direction of the offered goodies and slowly took the first step towards the source of the smell. I was rooted to the spot as I watched Hercules draw closer towards Andy's outstretched hand. Then he was there. Out popped his little pink tongue and he hungrily got stuck into the proffered peace offering.

It all seemed too easy, and, sure enough, once the titbit was finished, the sharp white teeth – now bigger than the last time – were again sunk into Andy's hand of friendship.

Andy's free hand delivered a sharp smack on Hercules's snout and he quickly dropped his second 'snack', now very bloody, with a look of amazement. It was to be the first of many battles with the wild young creature.

As autumn turned to winter we came to understand the tenacious instinct for survival in our growing friend. Each day was spent planning and working around Hercules, trying to overcome every setback as we came upon it. After the bout with Terrible Ted in Canada, Andy had sought out the bear's trainer, Gene DuBois and had learned a lot about the likes and dislikes of bears. Also he had been continually told of their innate treachery as a species.

Andy's physical strength and agility, and his wrestling background, made him better able to dodge the swift snaps and buffets aimed at him by the young bear and very gradually his courage and kindness seemed to get through to the suspicious young creature and win a glimmer of respect.

It was two months before I could even dare to touch him, and even then I had to withdraw from him very quickly before I had my hand mauled. It was a time of slow progress and many disappointments.

One of the earliest problems was to persuade Hercules to wear a collar and lead. It was like breaking in a stallion with very sharp teeth. Andy would move in as close as he could and catch him with a lasso. Hercules would tense his neck and dash about the den knocking Andy from wall to wall and diving in as often as possible to bite any part that he could reach. It was only superhuman determination that prevented Andy from giving up at this stage, but he knew that the moment Hercules felt he had the upper hand all that he had achieved so far would be lost.

No sooner was this hurdle cleared than we had to embark on the even more difficult task of persuading Hercules to wear a muzzle. He wouldn't have to wear it all the time – only when he was wrestling – but it was important to get him used to it as early as possible, and he was now nine months old. All those who had trained bears said that this had been too late to start but we had no alternative and ploughed on hopefully.

The first thing was, to have a muzzle made that fitted him properly. There were no handy manuals or textbooks to offer us guidance in this. It was a case of trial and error. The first muzzle was made of leather and consisted of a strap round Hercules's neck joined to two other straps around his nose that hung fairly loose. This was to get him used to the idea of having a 'bridle' on. To put it on him was a matter of bribery in the form of ice cream, grapes and yogurt, and very quick reflexes when he decided he'd rather have a bite at our arms instead.

We continued this for about a month, and only after this time would he allow us to work about his head, slipping the muzzle on and off without fuss.

In December it began to snow. Hercules had been with us now for four months, and, when we looked out of the window that morning after the first snowfall, we saw him happily burrowing his way under the deep snowdrifts in his den. I made breakfast of porridge and cream for Andy and me, and a great pot of beans, eggs, cod-liver oil and bread for Hercules. We topped this off with a large pot of tea with milk and sugar for all of us, and we were all ready to start the day. Hercules rushed out of his den and followed us into the paddock on his long lead, rushing about, madly diving into snow drifts until all you could see was his little furry bottom sticking up in the air against the brilliant white of the snow.

One of his favourite pastimes in the snow was sledging. He learned the skill accidentally on a large plastic container that he found in the paddock, discovering that if he placed his big front paws on it he could then push at the ground with his back paws and slide easily down the hill.

By the early spring we really thought we had a chance of proving the experts wrong. Not only was Hercules still with us, but we seemed to be making daily progress in our relationship with him. It's true that he was by no means a household pet – it was not our intention to turn him into one – but neither was he the fierce creature that he had been when he arrived, as most bears in captivity remained.

From the beginning of the 'experiment' the press had taken an interest, and they kept an eye open for developments as the months went by, tending to dwell on setbacks rather than achievements. There was, sadly, never any shortage of people to criticise and complain of danger. They usually took the line that it was for our own benefit, that we didn't know what we were doing, that we had no training in the handling of dangerous animals, that sooner or later there would be a fatal accident. In spite of it all we persevered; they could do little to harm us – or so we thought.

It was necessary for us to obtain two licences to keep Hercules: a Performing Animals Licence, which would enable us to train him and to entertain others with him; and the Dangerous Wild Animals Licence, a new licence introduced in April 1977, which would enable us to keep an animal specified under the Act that introduced it.

The first licence could be obtained only if the keeper had some experience of working with the animal in question and could show that his treatment of the animal and the conditions under which the beast was kept fulfilled the legal requirements. Local police and vets who had carefully monitored us since before Hercules's arrival lent their support to the application and the licence was obtained without any difficulty.

The second was a different matter. Because it was a new piece of legislation, the local council was unsure of how stringent it should be, and, since we were the guinea pigs, it wanted to make absolutely sure.

Although we had not seen a copy of the Act, we were told that it applied to us and were asked to send off details of the size of Hercules's den, the strength of the material it was built from, the number of warning notices about the place and so on. We were well above the required standards and supposed that it would simply be a matter of time before the necessary piece of paper arrived.

We were wrong. Stirling Council met once every fortnight and at meeting after meeting the application came up and was referred for further information. We couldn't believe it. Andy wrote to the authority suggesting that the surest way of judging was for members to visit the Sheriffmuir Inn and see for themselves, but they declined, preferring to continue 'considering' and 'referring' from the council chamber.

By this time it was becoming ridiculous and beginning to attract the attention of the local papers. It seemed that, although the council could not find any legal grounds for refusing the licence, there were several councillors who did not like the idea of a grizzly bear roaming about the hills of Sheriffmuir and were determined not to be rushed into any decision. After several months even the councillors were looking for a way out and decided to visit the Inn.

We were given pre-emptory notice of this and then were plagued at all hours of the day by the comings and goings of councillors, arriving without appointment and expecting to be shown round and given the full treatment.

We both felt irritated that these bureaucrats could arrive and roam about our home pulling at bars, opening doors and measuring things that had all been tested and measured before. Matters came to a head one Sunday with the arrival of a woman councillor.

I had been working hard in the bar all week and was

enjoying a peaceful afternoon mucking out the horses. I was about to go for a ride across the moors when I noticed a heavily made-up elderly woman in an imitation fur coat making across the yard and boldly opening the gate.

'Can I help you?' I asked.

'I'm from the council,' she said. 'I've come to see your bear.'

I closed the gate and followed her to Hercules's den.

'There he is,' I said, 'that's my baby.'

She looked at me as if I was mad and, hauling the plan of the enclosure from her bag, proceeded to walk round the den checking and testing things. As I watched her I could not fail to be struck by the contrast between the natural grace of the wild creature behind the bars and the phoney elegance of the human outside. A comparison between their coats made me smile involuntarily – the one so rich and glossy, the other so dull and tawdry. At that moment Andy arrived on the scene. I grimaced at him to let him know that something was up.

'Can I help you?' he asked.

'I'm from the council. I'm here to see your bear,' she said again.

'What do you think of him? He's a beautiful boy, isn't he?' asked Andy.

'No comment,' was all she said.

'I beg your pardon . . .' began Andy. I slid away to avoid the explosion. Where Hercules was concerned he reacted as most fathers would.

From the kitchen I saw the councillor wither under

Andy's broadside and the next minute she was in the bar, dragging away an astonished man from his half-pint.

'I'll not have you drinking in this place,' she said as she hurried him into her car and drove off, scattering stones.

CHAPTER 4

GROWING TRUST

It seemed miraculous to the doubters that within five months of Hercules coming to live with us we were confident enough in him to be able to accept an invitation to present him in public.

The invitation came from the promoters of the film *Grizzly*, which was to be premiered at the Odeon Cinema in Edinburgh in January 1977. The film was about a ferocious killer bear in the Rocky Mountains that attacked and ravished unsuspecting campers, and they wanted Hercules to perform the opening ceremony and take part in the press reception afterwards – he was sure to be a big draw.

The roads were clear of snow and we took Hercules down in the horsebox on the morning of the engagement. He seemed to catch our excitement and was eager for this new adventure, remaining unperturbed by even the strange noises of his first visit to the city. We didn't know where the cinema was and asked the way from a couple of pedestrians; once we had found it we were met by a police escort. Understandably nobody was taking any chances.

They directed us into a car park near the venue and stood about apprehensively while we checked that the cinema was suitable for Hercules. What they would have done if he had run amok I didn't ask. They later told me that they did not for a moment expect that they would be prepared to allow Hercules to mingle with the public.

We returned to the car park and dropped the ramp. Two inquisitive brown eyes sparkled in the gloom. Andy went into the box, clipped on the lead and, giving the thumbs-up, led Hercules out into the car park.

Surrounded by police officers, we walked up a brick-lined corridor and entered the theatre by a door right underneath the huge screen. The audience no doubt expected a blood-thirsty monster like the bear in the film; but they saw a large bear cub shyly blinking at the spotlights, and then intelligently he gained his confidence. Andy winked at me and I uncrossed my fingers. All would be well.

It went better than 'well': it was a resounding success. Hercules behaved like a young film star and gambolled happily up the aisle, looking for stray sweeties and smiling at the delighted audience.

We led him into the foyer at the front of the house, where there was already a small crowd of interested onlookers. Hercules played up to them and made a beeline for a large cardboard cutout of the fierce star of the movie. He considered it carefully and explored behind it and then, to the delight of the onlookers, proceeded to flatten it and pull it to pieces. It was all done in such a playful way that it seemed as if our young friend was clearly saying, '*I'm* the star of this show! What do you think *you're* doing here?'

Onlookers and police roared with laughter. I went over to one of the policemen who had escorted us and asked his verdict: 'He's been a perfect gentleman,' came the reply. 'Indeed, I've seen many a worse behaved dog. I think we can quite safely go home now.'

I turned and looked proudly at my two boys capering in front of their admirers.

We were greatly relieved that the event had gone off so well and, as we drove away from the Odeon, we felt very proud of our baby, now napping in the horsebox behind us with a belly full of ice cream and shandy. We stopped on the outskirts of Edinburgh to buy an evening paper, and to our surprise saw Hercules's broad face looking out at us from the front page. The press had pronounced the show a triumph.

As we drove further north the snow began to fall heavily again and by the time we reached the small road to our home it was clear that we were not going to be able to make it, towing the horsebox. We pulled into Sandy Anderson's farm road and unhitched the trailer. 'What about Hercules?' I asked Andy. 'We'll take him in the car with us,' he replied. 'It'll be better than walking on a night like this, and we have only three miles to go.'

'Do you think that's wise?'

It wasn't. As soon as he was in the van Hercules lunged towards the front seats. I leapt out to safety while Andy tried to comfort the startled bear. There was nothing for it but to walk, and, as soon as he was in the open air, Hercules happily entered into the spirit of the thing. I drove the van on ahead and put the kettle on. As they came to the road end I watched with apprehension as Andy leaned down and loosed the leash. I need not have worried. I gave a shout, Hercules pricked up his ears and bounded right into his den.

We all three drank mugs of tea and congratulated each other on a most successful day.

The snow fell for three days that week and the three of us were snowbound. It was a time of marvellous companionship and growing awareness of the powerful bond that was forming between us. We were able to let Hercules wander about without his lead as the snow was so deep that it made even him timid. He liked to feel in control of situations and he became concerned if he suddenly disappeared in a snowdrift or had to bulldoze his way too far from the security of his warm den.

Winter turned into spring. My horses were back out in the paddock, frisky as they sensed the sap rising. They had been previously aware of Hercules from the start and we had made sure that they were kept well apart. 'Horses and bears don't mix,' said the books. 'Horses have a deep-rooted, primeval fear of bears.' In time, however, we decided to put these theories to the test.

At first the horses took to their heels whenever he came

into sight. After each burst of speed they'd stop and turn to face the furry shape, which always seemed to be able to corner them, even in the twenty-acre field. They stared towards it and their nostrils flared until the shape grew too close for comfort, and once more they'd be off. Hercules couldn't understand this behaviour. He seemed puzzled by the fact that these creatures just didn't seem to want his friendship and preferred to retreat, leaving him to wonder why his efforts to become friends weren't working. But daily cavorting paid off in the end.

Sheriffmuir, a superb jumper full of guts and more intelligence than I have ever known in any other horse, became particularly aware of this persistent fellow who shared his field for an hour or so each day, and began to develop a special bond with him. It happened gradually. They weighed each other up and seemed to think out each step carefully as they approached the imagined barrier that had separated them so far. Sheriffmuir knew he had speed as his trump card, just in case.

Hercules, for his part, seemed to acknowledge that the spindly bay didn't fear him and slowed down his movements when the little horse with the intelligent eyes came near. He seemed to sense that this was one he could get through to – a friend for the future, perhaps. We watched the two of them daily coming closer together, stealthily moving, until at last one sunny day they came nose to nose.

Sheriffmuir's tense neck lowered to greet the outstretched, black button nose that Hercules offered. A quick sniff, a little snort, and Sheriffmuir backed away a step or two, waiting, gingerly to see the reaction of the strange animal. Hercules seemed to sense that this was his chance to let the horse see that he meant no harm. He stood motionless, trying in his own way to communicate confidence to the other noble head that watched him cautiously from a few feet away. Andy and I stood rooted to the spot, trying to keep our excitement under control. 'What a beautiful sight,' I thought with pride welling up inside me as we waited for the next move.

Hercules's tactics were working. Sheriffmuir sensed that the outstretched nose was an offer of friendship and slowly stepped forward for another reassuring sniff.

Hercules sniffed back and then out came that long pink and black tongue to give the soft muzzle a great big lick to seal the bond. At last Hercules had made his point and won the confidence of the shy horses.

From that day on Hercules's understanding of the timorous nature of his gentle friends grew. He often accompanied me as I schooled them and occasionally tried his skill over the small jumps I erected for him. He invariably ended up by mashing them into firewood!

Hercules was very possessive of Andy and me, and, although he had become used to the horses, he was put out if he thought we were paying too much attention to them, and he'd show his displeasure by crying loudly and thumping his heavy metal pot on the ground until the noise became too much to bear and we gave in and would go and play with him for a spell.

We were aware of this when Allan, a friend who helped

in the hotel, arrived with an accidental litter of kittens that he could not possibly keep in his small house in Dunblane. He asked if we could keep them and try to find permanent homes for them. If we couldn't, they would have to be drowned.

They moved in, but by late afternoon one of the litter – a little white bundle of fluff – looked unhappy and we brought her indoors. Hercules was perplexed by what was going on and sat sniffing at the wall that separated his den from the hay shed. When we brought the tiny white creature into the kitchen he started acting up, diving about his den and peering excitedly through the kitchen window to spot its exact whereabouts. We settled the little kitten in front of the fire and hoped that Hercules would settle down too, but, when the strange white creature didn't reappear from his kitchen, Hercules sat dejectedly for a moment and then started to cry. His cry sounded just as if he were saying 'mom' over and over again.

'You'll have to take the wee thing out, Maggie,' said Andy. 'Hercules is jealous. He thinks his mum and dad have found someone else and he feels left out.' I picked up the kitten and carried him back to the others. Hercules seemed more than satisfied. He stopped his crying and swaggered round his den – once more he had made his point.

Then one morning, as I was washing up the breakfast dishes, I saw the mischievous little kitten disappear through the entrance to Hercules's inner den. I knew Hercules was inside on his bed of sawdust and rushed out to try to divert the little creature from certain disaster.

I slid back the side door to the main den and reached the inner door in time to see Hercules raise a massive paw and bring it down on top of the tiny unconcerned creature. I was about to cry out but then checked myself as I realised that he had halted his paw within fractions of an inch of the kitten's back and was feeling it very gently. He often did this to things — for example, he liked to run his paw gently round the contours of our faces — but I never expected that he would have such control over his immense strength that he could avoid crushing a kitten.

The kitten rolled over on its back and pressed its little feet against the huge foot above it, enjoying the game, and thereafter it would fearlessly sneak into the den in search of fun.

Another animal that crept into Herc's inner sanctum was Charlie the pheasant. Charlie was a wild pheasant from the woods near by who had discovered that there were often tasty scraps to be had in the den. We saw him so often, stalking proudly about the enclosure, that we could recognise him and even christened him.

Herc didn't seem to mind him when he cheekily strolled into the inner den and pecked up food from right under his nose. Then one day Andy called me to the outer run and drew my attention to a mass of pheasant feathers. 'Looks like Hercules's finally had enough of cheeky Charlie.' Strangely, we could find no sign of Charlie's body and since Herc always refused to eat raw meat we doubted whether he had gobbled him up. It was a mystery.

And then, about three days later, who should emerge

from the den but a very shamefaced-looking Charlie – with hardly a feather on his body.

One would have thought that the terrified bird would have learned his lesson from such an experience, but not a bit of it. He returned even more frequently than before. We put grain out for him and he became quite tame. His feathers grew back again and we saw him almost every day.

We have often wondered what it could be that Charlie found to eat in the den – before we started putting out grain, that is. He must have been attracted by the hay in the barn, for there was not much in Herc's diet that would be good for pheasants, and, anyway, he left very little of what he was given to eat.

For breakfast we gave him between one and three dozen eggs (it depended on the time of year – he got more in summer – and on who fed him: Andy would spoil him); six tins of spaghetti hoops in tomato sauce and a loaf of bread. This was all washed down with a gallon of sweet, milky tea – and it must be milky, mind, or he would knock over the pail and demand more.

For lunch he had fruit – usually grapes and apples – and for dinner he had a main meal of cooked meat, with vegetables such as carrots, cabbage, or broccoli. The meat is often ox hearts cooked in tomato, lentil or oxtail soup, or, as a special treat, roast chicken, which was his favourite dish.

In summer he required about 15 pounds of meat *per meal*. We topped off the daily dinner with a whole bottle of advocaat, which he loved and which was very good for his coat. He also liked curries and spaghetti Bolognese, but, surprisingly enough, he was not terribly keen on honey.

His meals were served on a silver tray, which came by courtesy of Trust House Hotels. We were staying in one of these establishments and borrowed the tray to break Herc's breakfast eggs into. He enjoyed eating off it so much that, when Andy asked him to give it up, he wouldn't. Andy explained all this to the chef, who was angrily asking for his tray back. 'I'm afraid you'll have to get it from him yourself,' Andy said. 'Herc won't give it to me.' The chef left his kitchen and came out to the truck. I don't think he had really believed it when he had been told that we wanted the tray to feed a bear, because, when he was confronted by a nearly full-grown grizzly, weighing over 40 stone, he nearly fainted. Andy introduced them and Hercules was very friendly but adamant about his tray. The chef kindly gave it to him as a present.

When Hercules was not much more than a year old we decided that we must buy him his own truck. Sharing a trailer with horses was not good enough, and, anyway, he would soon be too big for the horsebox. We thought that it would be more pleasant for him if he were able to see what was going on, and, after long consultations with our local blacksmith, Bob Burnett, Andy decided to buy a Toyota pickup truck onto the back of which Bob could fit a cage.

When it was done it looked very smart indeed. It remained to be seen whether Hercules would like it. He approached cautiously and sniffed the suspicious new thing and it took some time to coax him into the cage itself. We left him to sit in the sun for an hour or so, and acclimatise himself to his new travelling den, and then Andy drove gently down the road. At first Hercules jumped about and rocked the truck frantically, but then he settled down and took up a position standing on his hind legs behind the driver in order to watch where they were going. From then on he always took up this position in the Toyota.

As we travelled about further afield with Hercules, it became necessary to get an even bigger 'travelling den' for him. We decided the best thing would be to secure a second-hand single-decker bus and convert it into accommodation for both ourselves and Hercules.

It didn't look much that first day we saw it, neglected and scruffy-looking with its panels painted a drab blue and inside showing signs of much wear and tear. But its engine had a steady beat and we drove it home full of plans for renovation. A complete facelift was called for and so we set about working on it through the cold days and long nights of the winter. Herc didn't like it at all. We tried to persuade him to have a look inside and told him it would be his new travelling den, but he would have none of it and wouldn't come within 20 feet of the bus. It was clearly going to be a struggle to persuade him into it.

First the seats had to come out to make way for the den in the back compartment and a living area in front for us. Then the exterior of the coach was buffed down to the bare metal to give a base for the new colours it was to be painted in: bright red on a cream base with lots of stars and fancy lettering. The inside was plush and comfortable. The last job of all was the fitting of a bright new wire-mesh cage from the blacksmith's.

It looked sensational when Andy drove it into the yard. Now to see what Herc thought.

The cage at the back seemed to give him confidence, or maybe he just liked the bright colours, for he walked boldly up to his new caravan and, after sniffing around it for a few moments, stood up on the stair leading into our living room and peered at it from the safety of the bottom step. Then he jumped in and investigated. Having done this he was more than happy to check out his cage, and sat in it with a proprietorial air.

When Hercules became a household name we bought yet another bus to transport him about the place. This one was made especially for him and us, and had every conceivable mod-con.

Having a travelling home for the three of us became necessary from early on. When Hercules was only a year and a half old Andy had to go away for a couple of days. The whole time he was away Herc did nothing but lie morosely in his den, moping and wondering where his pal had gone. I did my best to cheer him up with some of his favourite snacks, but, after he had greedily swallowed them, he lapsed back into his black mood.

The first thing Andy did on his return was to visit his chum, but Herc would have none of it. He felt that he hadn't been consulted and that accordingly he had every right to be moody. It took a lot of sweet-talking on Andy's part to coax him out of his huff.

On another occasion we both decided that we deserved a short holiday. Our friend Allan agreed to look after the Inn and take care of Herc for the three days that we planned to be away, and we towed a small speedboat, which we had rather obviously named *Bearpower*, up to Loch Etive with the intention of exploring the coast.

The hotel was in a beautiful location, the staff were very kind and our room was comfortable. After unpacking we went down to the loch to launch the boat and then returned to our room to shower before dinner.

Although the food was good, and typically highland, our meal was a sombre affair and our conversation nonexistent. Without admitting it to each other we felt like a couple of traitors who had abandoned someone who needed us. We knew that Allan would take great care of Hercules, but we remembered Herc's moodiness when Andy was away and couldn't bear to think of him sitting morosely in his den, wondering where we were.

By the end of the meal we were utterly miserable and in the very opposite of a holiday mood. I telephoned Allan, with Andy standing beside me listening to what he said. It was clear that Hercules was as miserable as we were. There was no point in staying any longer, for what value was a holiday if you spent it wishing you were elsewhere?

We left first thing the next day and, as soon as we arrived back, went straight to see Hercules. His black mood this time was twice as bad as his huff on the last occasion, and we had to spend at least half an hour bribing him with sweeties in the sitting room before he regained his usual cheerful mood.

After this we decided that, whenever we went on holiday in future, we would have to take Hercules with us. He was as much a member of the family as any vulnerable child would be – and a very jealous child at that.

We knew that Hercules felt that we belonged to him as much as he belonged to us. He was prepared to share us with others occasionally, just as we were prepared to share him, but only on the strict understanding that it was temporary and that we would quickly revert to our close family role. I was often asked whether I planned to have children and Andy and I had talked about this at length. The conclusion we reached, and the answer I gave, was that Hercules would regard another member of the family as a betrayal of the very special and singular relationship that we had built up. It was a massive commitment but one that felt right for us.

After all, what is a successful family but a close group of individuals who love and depend upon one another? Children grow up and leave the nest and find loved ones and people to depend on elsewhere. Hercules had only us and we were proud to shoulder the responsibility of his love, for God willing, the next forty years.

CHAPTER 5

KINGS OF
THE RING

Andy's first encounter with a bear had been in the ring, and from the start his hope was to share his love of wrestling with our adopted son. Hercules needed no encouragement – after all, the sport originated among Native Americans watching the antics of bears in the wild. The difficulty would be to prevent him being carried away with enthusiasm so that he would use his full strength, and either accidentally or in a fit of pique snap Andy's back or give him a swipe that would brain him.

Herc's sheer bulk and strength meant that Andy had to use all his might and the skill gained from years in the ring to keep up with him and gradually teach him about human limitations. Beginning with casual rough-and-tumbles, he was gradually able to employ more complicated wrestling moves and to teach Hercules what fun it could be to slip out of a hold and put his human opponent on the defensive. Everything depended on building up Herc's trust and making him realise that the very last thing in the world Andy wanted to do was to harm him. It required great patience and delicacy, for Hercules was acutely suspicious of every new move.

One day they were wrestling in the snow – by this time Herc was fairly addicted to the sport – and Andy was tempted to put the 'scissors' round his sparring partner's neck, a move he had not tried before. In doing so he accidentally clonked Hercules on the top of the head. Hercules immediately sprang free and ran to me for protection and comfort, pressing into the back of my legs and using me as a shield to ward off the formidable Andy! It was one of the tenderest moments I think I have ever experienced. He was just like a confused and frightened child, running to his mum for protection. Andy spoke softly to him, kept reassuring him and repeating, 'I'm sorry, baby, I'm sorry,' while Hercules peered nervously over his shoulder. After a while they made up. Herc's faith was restored and they resumed their game.

It was some time, and only after a lot of careful training, before Andy was again allowed to put the 'scissors' on, and by that time Hercules was so accomplished a wrestler that he didn't take long to break the hold.

As Herc's confidence and trust in us grew he took great pleasure in showing off his prowess as a wrestler before an audience. Every Saturday, once our guests at the Inn had finished their supper, we invited them to move up to the top part of the lounge so that we could clear the lower part in readiness for a most unusual cabaret.

Once all was ready, in would trot Andy and Hercules – the latter delighted and excited by the chatter and laughter from his admirers. The noise soon abated, however, once the pair started their act, rolling about the floor, grunting and groaning in fine style. The audience were spellbound as first one then the other champion managed to take the upper hand. It was quite clear, though, whom they supported, and, as Herc warmed to the sport and pinned his opponent to the mat, waiting for the count of three, spontaneous applause and laughter rang out.

It was hot work tumbling about with a half-grown bear in front of a roaring log fire, and, after a short while, the round would end and drinks would be served to the contestants, to the delight and amusement of our guests. Herc would comfortably sit back on his haunches and quickly down a pint of his favourite tipple, lemonade shandy, held expertly between his massive front paws. A proper gent.

One particularly strenuous night Hercules was eager for more than his customary pint. Another was fetched for him and still his thirst was not quenched. After a couple more he was satisfied and ready to return to his den. He appeared to be unaffected by his overindulgence – except for a mischievous grin and a certain bleariness about his eyes – but, when we reached the cold fresh air at the kitchen door, his legs simply buckled under him and down he went. He, of course, was very contented with the situation, lying on his back on the kitchen floor waving his legs happily in the air. Our problem was how to manoeuvre the giant bulk of a bear back to his bed. It took ages, but, stumble by stumble, we made it and one boozy bear was safely tucked up to sleep the sleep of the just. The next morning he looked distinctly hung-over.

As Herc grew bigger it became impossible to continue with these Saturday-evening demonstrations in the small lounge, but by this time the pair were training for Hercules's first professional contest, which was to be held in Perth in August 1977.

The summer weather was perfect for the long runs and exercise bouts that filled the month before the great day. Astonished drivers on the Sheriffmuir road would see man and beast embracing by the roadside, Herc with his massive arms wrapped round Andy's muscular shoulders, or perhaps gently tracing the contours of Andy's face with his huge paw as they rested after a strenuous workout. Cars would pull up, small traffic jams would form. Groups of unbelieving motorists would approach to within what they considered to be a safe distance and fire questions at the pair. Andy would enthusiastically reply on behalf of both of them and Herc would grin good-naturedly.

As the month of intensive training went by, Herc became more and more adept at the game. Now, each time Andy tried a new manoeuvre, his companion seemed to consider it carefully, and, invariably, by the time Andy tried it again, he had thought of a countermove. Indeed, such was Herc's intelligence that he began to invent his own holds and to employ them with great gusto – to the considerable discomfort of his sparring partner.

Although the relationship that had developed between the two was so close and affectionate, Andy was by no means blind to the dangers of wrestling with a grizzly bear. As Hercules developed his muscles and became heavier, so Andy had to trim his weight down and build his strength up so that, in the event of something untoward happening, he could jump clear. Even the backs of strong men were like matchsticks to the powerful bear.

As well as the physical preparation of the contestants we had to devise some way of preventing Herc from rolling between the ropes and out of the ring during the fight. We had noticed that whenever he felt unsure of things – strange noises or traffic, for example – he liked to retreat into his den or into the pickup truck that we transported him in and stay there until the danger had passed. (This in itself gives the lie to the popular belief that bears are ferocious aggressors and will attack without thinking. Rather, they know that survival depends upon not risking the unknown, avoiding it if they possibly can, attacking only if cornered and desperate.)

In the end we decided to construct a low, lightweight wire fence that could be erected in sections round the ring. This turned out to be a great success for, while leaving the crowd's view uninterrupted, it seemed to give Hercules a feeling of security, and security was particularly necessary on this occasion as the contest was to be held indoors, in the Perth ice rink, and Herc was used to fighting in the open air.

We set off early, Andy driving the pickup with Hercules and me following in the Volkswagen, towing the horsebox for him to rest in privacy. But when he arrived, Hercules would have none of it and, after posing for photographers for half an hour, he stubbornly refused to nap in the horsebox. He wasn't going to miss anything, and, after all, he was the star of the show and every whim must be pandered to. So he stood in the pickup in the slow drizzle, watching everything that was going on with keen interest, as the audience arrived and an expectant murmur rose from within the rink.

It was to be a five-bout spectacular. The first act warmed the audience up, and the second was between two attractive girls who quickly showed the spectators that they were more than just pretty faces and gave an excellent account of themselves. By the interval the audience were in a good mood and the air of expectancy for what was to come had reached fever pitch. We brought Hercules from the truck to his dressing room under the grandstand and he nervously looked about him and up at the ceiling, which was reverberating with the excited stamping of the spectators. I had made some tea and hoped that this, and some of the grapes that he loved so much, would reassure him that there was nothing to be afraid of. The moment of truth would come five minutes later when we had to encourage the young fellow to allow us to muzzle him.

He hated this, and would allow Andy to do it only when he was calm and confident. That evening he was shy and jumpy and with every glance at the ceiling my hopes that he would allow us to put the thing on dwindled. My heart was pounding, my throat was dry and my hands were shaking. While I comforted him and fed him grapes, Andy slipped his collar on. All I could think about was the hundreds of people out there who had come especially to see my two men do their stuff. How awful it would be if we let them down. I was oblivious to everything in the room except for the muzzle in my crazily shaking hands as I petted him and comforted him, and Andy soothed him with, 'It's all right, old son. It's going to be fun. You have friends out there.'

Herc stared about, unconcerned, and then quite suddenly lowered his big wet nose and allowed Andy to strap on the hated muzzle. All would be well – Herc had come up trumps again. I squeezed my man's hand and hugged my big baby, the latter looking at me as if to say, 'What's all the fuss about? I'm a professional. You don't think I'd let you down, do you?'

I went out into the stadium and heard the master of ceremonies announcing that there would be a five-minute break before the main event to allow for the fence to be erected.

'The event you are about to watch,' I heard his voice echoing tinnily through the stadium, 'is unique in the history of wrestling. Not only will Andy Robin attempt to go fifteen minutes with a grizzly bear and thus create a new world record – the previous record is a mere five minutes – but he will do this without the bear being attached to a restraining rope. No one has ever risked this before. The danger is so great and the strength of these creatures so immense that there has always been a handler in the ring with the animal, and the animal has always been restrained by a rope and choker so that it can be dragged off when things go wrong.

'In spite of this,' he continued, 'tragedies abound. You may recall the tragic occasion when Jimmy Chipperfield, one of the most respected bear experts of modern times, attempted to wrestle with Bruno the Bear back in 1935 in the London Palladium. Mr Chipperfield lost a lung after only four minutes . . .'

I needed no reminding as the adrenalin coursed through my veins. I prayed silently that Hercules would not forget himself in the excitement and would control his will to win.

'I must ask you to remain absolutely silent, ladies and gentlemen, until Hercules has entered the ring. Are we ready?' He turned to the men putting up the fence. 'Ladies and gentlemen, it is my pleasure to introduce to you Grizzly Andy Robin and Hercules the Bear.'

There was an awed silence. I hurried back to the dressing room to tell the boys the curtain was up. They were deep in consultation, Andy with his arm round Herc's shoulders, Hercules with his chin on Andy's knees.

As we walked towards the ring, our hollow-sounding footsteps were the only noise to be heard. Herc walked beside Andy with his body pressed tightly against his master's legs for reassurance, his brown eyes darting this way and that, taking in his surroundings, watching the pale faces of the spectators craning to catch a glimpse of him.

When he saw the familiar ring he walked eagerly towards it and jumped like an old pro straight through the ropes and

Above: Sheriffmuir Inn, Perthshire.

Below: Eddie Orbell with Baby Hercules.

Above: Andy gets the upper hand in a bout from his wrestling days.

Below: Maggie the showjumper.

Below right: Woodsman at work!

Left: Andy's great strength becomes apparent.

Below: So many happy days together.   (*Aberdeen Journals Ltd*)

Time I had a bigger bath!

Right: My young Herc.

Left: Dad and me in training.
(*Cinécosse Film Television and Audio-Visual Production*)

Right: Filming with Cinécosse – two handsome young men.
(*Cinécosse Film Television and Audio-Visual Production*)

Left: Wandering over the moors.

Right: Hercules makes his first public appearance (Andy's dad in flat cap).
(*Whyler Workrooms*)

Left: Hmm – we like our beautiful new travelling home. (*Glasgow Herald*)

Above: Utterly dejected and exhausted.

Below: The two crofters who spotted Hercules with a very wet Andy.
(*Daily Star*)

Right: Hercules is chased by Eddie Orbell and the vet. (*Alan Mann Helicopters Ltd*)

Left: The drugged Hercules is transported in a net beneath the helicopter.

(*Peter Stone/Mirrorpix*)

Right: Unceremoniously bundled from the helicopter.

onto the floor of the ring, where he turned to his partner as if to say, 'Come on, then, what are you waiting for?' I shut the gate in the fence and took my seat.

Andy picked up the microphone to say a few introductory words, but Hercules would have none of it. He bounded across the ring, reared up on his hind legs and tackled Andy from behind, almost causing him to swallow the mike. The fight was on.

Hercules's talent that night was a joy to watch. With intuitive intelligence and elegant skill he escaped from all the holds that Andy put him into. Then he would take the lead and pin Andy to the canvas. The crowd roared their applause. But, with his agility and experience, Andy would manage to break free from his giant opponent, only to be knocked to the floor once more.

Hercules was enjoying every minute and would look up now and then to make sure he was receiving the attention he deserved from the spectators. Then he turned back to the fight and proudly headbutted Andy across the ring, to the delight of the audience. Once Andy had recovered from this setback he resumed the offensive and tried to throw Hercules over his leg, but his opponent was too wily, and dexterously shifted his feet back and forth without even glancing down, seeming to know by intuition which leg Andy was aiming for, and lifted it out of reach before he could get at it.

'Ten minutes' rang out through the PA system.

The sweat ran off Andy in silver rivulets under the spotlights and even Hercules was beginning to pant a little.

Neither was in the mood to give up, though, and Hercules was as determined to win as Andy was to avoid being crushed. Only a minute to go. I could slacken my grip on the pint of shandy I was clutching as I realised that everything had gone perfectly according to plan and the danger was almost past. The bell rang. It was over. The bout was pronounced a draw and the world record was well and truly broken.

As one, the crowd rose and gave my boys a standing ovation. Months of work and worry now seemed worthwhile. Andy undid Hercules's leather muzzle and handed him the well-deserved pint. Hercules had already spotted it and sat down on the canvas in anticipation – it was gone in moments.

By now the crowd had surged round the ring, shouting congratulations and asking questions. One of the first there was Eddie Orbell from the Wildlife Park at Kincraig. 'Well done, Andy!' he said. 'Hercules is in beautiful condition. I never thought you'd manage it. I thought I'd have him back in the park within a week.'

The press were also there, looking, I thought, somewhat disappointed. I was later told by a friendly journalist that they had come to see Andy killed!

The Perth ice rink event had highlighted the problem of having to have Hercules muzzled during wrestling bouts. At first we thought it was only a temporary thing, and that he would get used to his muzzle again before too long, but as time went on, it was clear that he was not going to change his attitude towards it.

On such occasions as he allowed us to put it on him, as in Perth, usually now by breaking a couple of eggs into it by way of a bribe, he looked at us as if to say, 'Our relationship is based on trust, and yet you do not fully trust me.' We dared not. When wrestling in the wild, bears use their teeth to haul each other about, catching hold of each other's tough, loose pelt and using the hold thus gained as a levering point. Hercules could not be expected to realise that human skin is no protection against two-inch-long teeth and Andy would have been, at least, terribly scarred. Indeed, in the thrill of a bout Hercules could easily have become so carried away that even worse might happen. But in the months following the Perth event he became more and more reluctant to have the thing put on him, until he devised a way of beating us at our own game.

The way was very simple: he would not wrestle. He would sit on his haunches in the corner looking imperiously about him, sulking openly. No begging or bribing would persuade him to shift. It reached the stage where we could not rely on him to even play up to his audience.

He would just act as if he didn't know what was going on and he would often search me out from the crowd with his eyes and look to me for support in the stand he was making.

One day his resistance to the muzzle became active rather than passive and Andy narrowly escaped a very hard beating. It was during a bout in Dumfries in the spring of 1978, about eight months after the Perth event. Andy and Herc were billed to wrestle and they had attracted a large crowd to the Loreburn Hall. We had managed to persuade Hercules to put on his muzzle by breaking an egg into it, but he was particularly listless and it had taken an unusually long time to get it on. Both of us were apprehensive in case he played up. And, sure enough, once he was in the ring, he wandered about morosely and would not be enticed into wrestling.

Andy had explained to the audience that, unlike many other animals, Hercules was not simply conditioned to perform. If he didn't want to fight, he wouldn't and that was all there was to it. The audience would get their money back.

He tried all Hercules's favourite moves, offering him grapes and pleading with him, but Hercules was surly and unhelpful, wanting all the time to come over to me outside the ring. Then, quite suddenly, he seemed to think, 'To hell with this! I'll show him I mean business.' And, rearing up on his hind legs, he tried to clout Andy so hard that it would have smashed his skull. Andy dodged and realised immediately from the look in Herc's eye that this was for real. He wasn't trying to do Andy serious injury, but he was determined to make his point, and when bears do that they are certain to do serious injury.

The next seven or eight minutes were very tense as Andy tried to dodge and calm Hercules down. At last he succeeded and he turned to the audience to apologise that there would be no wrestling that day and to offer them their money back. The audience, however, were delighted with the show. They had not realised that Hercules had been seriously trying to injure his partner and that Andy had been seriously trying to keep out of his way, and felt they had *had* their money's worth.

It brought to a head, though, Andy's and my concern about muzzling our friend.

Hercules was far more to us than a way of making money. He was far more to us than a pet. He was far more to us than proof of a successful zoological experiment in animal–human relationships. He was a friend, a beloved companion – a son.

We loved him more than anything else in the world. Our lives were intertwined even more than the lives of many members of a family. We could not bear to see him unhappy.

Andy loved wrestling, and so did Hercules for that matter, and without the muzzle this pleasure, and considerable financial benefits that it brought, would have to be sacrificed. Our relationship was based on complete trust, the muzzle was a breach of that trust, and Hercules might understandably be suspicious of other things if this breach was not filled.

It did not surprise me when Andy came into the kitchen one morning, took down the muzzle and put it away. Our boy meant too much to us to be exploited in this way.

Hercules seemed to realise that we had made this decision and vindicated it completely by showering us with affection. In the months that followed we became inseparable, romping and playing and swimming and walking. There was no doubt in our minds that we had done the right thing.

Three months later we decided to make a film with Hercules, to be called *Hercules: Our Wrestling Bear*. It was to be based on a typical day in his life.

After some investigations we finally fixed upon a company called Cinécosse and commissioned them to make the film. They had no idea what they were letting themselves in for, but they were delighted by the project, had an open mind

and were ready for anything. Herc immediately took over –
unlike Andy and me, who self-consciously bungled our parts
for the first couple of days. He seemed to know exactly what
was required, entertaining the film crew with a continual
variety of comic antics, and beautifully upstaging Andy in
every scene. Mike Marshall, the director, and his crew were
delighted and, within twenty-four hours, had christened our
big baby 'One-take Herc'. Then came a hitch: Mike wanted
a wrestling scene as the centrepiece for the whole film. 'It's
crucial,' he said, 'unless you want to completely alter the
development of the movie and the title. You can't have a film
called *Our Wrestling Bear* without any wrestling in it!'

We explained the problem and said that it was impossible,
but he begged us to try it just once; such was his faith in
the hero of the film by this time that he was sure he would
oblige.

I would have bet everything I had that Hercules would
refuse to cooperate, and Andy felt the same. After all, it had
been so long and his dislike of the muzzle was too deep-
rooted. Andy approached the den with the thing in his hand
and I waited for Hercules to back off in disgust. Then, to
our amazement, the opposite happened. Up he came to his
partner eager to begin the business of the day – which he
was enjoying enormously, as it gave him lots of attention
and rewards and involved very little work – and then down
he sat and offered his big black nose to the muzzle.

We were astonished. All the way to the paddock where the
cameras were waiting Andy shook his head in amazement,
muttering, 'I don't believe it. I simply don't believe it.'

Hercules acted as if nothing had happened at all and gave an expert demonstration of his prowess, and as I watched him I couldn't help but wonder what was going on in that complex brain of his. He quite clearly and voluntarily had offered to put up with something he detested in order to help us out of a tricky situation. I felt profoundly moved.

The end of the muzzle saga was the most moving incident of all. Indeed, it proved a turning point in our whole relationship with our beloved boy – a turning point in the whole history of man's relationship with bears, come to that.

Two or three months after the film was finished, Andy and Hercules had been on a long walk in the hills and were running and swimming down in the river near the Inn. Andy was walking in the shallows by the bank and Hercules was playfully ambling close behind him. Suddenly, Andy slid on a stone and fell with a splash half on top of Herc. The latter immediately thought that his partner was starting another of their wrestling bouts, and, seizing the opportunity to score points, jumped on Andy before he could get up, pinning him to the ground with his great bulk and jamming his huge snout into Andy's neck. The blood drained from Andy's face as he thought, 'Well, this is it. He'll have my throat out now.' He was utterly helpless beneath the great bulk of Hercules's stomach. The pair looked at each other seriously, and mutual understanding was heavy in the gap between their eyes. Then Hercules jumped up and backed off to allow Andy to get to his feet – quite out of character in a wrestling bout. He stood motionless, watched his precious friend and master as if to say, 'Have I made my point?'

Andy ran hell for leather up to the house, eagerly pursued by Hercules, burst into the kitchen with tears in his eyes and joy in his face. *'Throw away that muzzle, Maggie, we'll never need it again!'*

I felt so proud of them both that I could have cried myself.

CHAPTER 6

STARRING ROLES

Some five months before the world record had been broken in Perth, Hercules obtained his first advertising job.

The promoters of Hofmeister lager had seen a photograph of Herc in a newspaper and asked if we would consider doing a promotional tour for their product, since its trademark was a bear. It was our first opportunity to show Hercules off south of the border, and we accepted the job eagerly. We knew he would do his stuff after the success of the premiere in Edinburgh, and we had the bright new pickup truck to take him down in.

There were to be five venues in all and the first was in Bournemouth. We drove down, towing a small wooden trailer full of provisions (the tour was going to last ten days) and were met by two representatives of the advertising agency and taken to the large nightclub where Hercules was to appear.

As we arrived at the stage door members of Suzi Quatro's band were unloading their gear. One of the roadies, glancing at Hercules as we led him in, said, 'Good suit that, innit? You can 'ardly tell the difference. Looks really real.' He couldn't believe it when Hercules later turned out to be the real thing.

At the door there was a large, muscle-bound bouncer in a smart blue suit. He was waiting for the first opportunity to throw troublemakers out. He looked strong and fearsome, but when he saw Hercules come lumbering along he seemed to go a shade paler and dashed off, howling 'Man, oh, man!'

The nightclub was very big, but the stage we had to use was tiny and almost covered with the promotional items. I hoped the place wouldn't be too crowded, so that we could use part of the dance floor, but, when I went onto the stage to introduce Andy and Hercules, I was dismayed to see it packed with young people in vivid disco gear. The music was very loud and for a moment my nerves got the better of me, but the show must go on and I asked them to make less noise, otherwise the bear they were about to meet would be scared off. Mercifully, they heeded my words. I think they believed they were going to see some sort of hoax.

Andy and Hercules came onto the stage, the former holding a juicy roast chicken to settle Hercules down with. You could have heard a pin drop as he considered the flushed faces peering at him in the semidarkness while he munched on his chicken. Then he relaxed and immediately started rolling on the floor. The audience were captivated and the girls started screaming as if he were a pop idol.

The rest of the tour went off without a hitch, although in Reading we had a bit of difficulty at our hotel. We were booked into Trust House Hotels wherever we went because they stood in their own grounds and there was plenty of greenery about. We were always given a ground-floor room so that we could back the truck right up to the window to reassure Hercules about his strange surroundings, and so that he could watch the television through our window. He was very fond of television, especially films that had a lot of action in them and cartoons (particularly *Tom and Jerry*).

We were getting ready for bed and Herc was quietly watching the television through the window when a frustrated night manageress knocked on our door.

'There's a couple upstairs who are not happy about sleeping with a bear under their window. They say they can't sleep. Could you possibly have a word with them and reassure them that he won't climb up and eat them during the night?'

'Away up and speak to them, Maggie,' said Andy. 'You're better at this sort of thing than I am.'

The manageress nervously took me up to the room and then hid behind me. I understood her nervousness when the door was opened by a large and angry lady in curlers covered by a pink hairnet.

'I believe you're concerned about our bear,' I began.

A bald-headed man with spectacles, who had forgotten to put in his false teeth, came up behind her.

'Damned ridiculous,' he hissed through his gums. 'We've been here for three days now and haven't had a decent night's sleep yet, what with the workmen banging away from first thing in the morning and now this bloody bear beneath our window. A bear! I ask you!'

They were furious, and beyond reasoning with. We went back downstairs, and, as the manageress left us, she said, 'I hope Hercules will go to sleep now and not bump about, or I'll have to move you to another room.'

As I got into bed I wondered what she could have meant. And then it started! Hercules had discovered that, by rocking his cage, he could make it clank against a roan pipe (the drainpipe leading down from the roof gutter) that ran past the angry couple's window and then, when he clanked, they came to the window to look daggers at him. He thought this was a great game and, although we told him to stop it, he was enjoying it too much, and, after keeping quiet for a moment or two, started up again.

The couple had obviously gone to bed and were not coming to the window, for after rattling around for a time Hercules became desperate to further alert their attention and started banging his heavy metal pot against the sides of the cage.

Later that summer we were contacted by the BBC, who were looking for a bear to take part in a film they were making for television, called *The Eagle of the Ninth*. The plot of the film centred on the Roman legion that disappeared in Scotland and was about the son of the commander of the lost legion setting out to solve the mystery.

It was being shot at Fintry in Stirlingshire and the idea was to use Hercules in a scene where he would be fighting with wolves – done by trick photography, of course. Two representatives of the BBC came up to Sheriffmuir. As soon as they met Hercules and saw what he could do, they changed the plan for the film and asked if Andy would take the part of a gladiator.

The day we were due to shoot the scene it poured with rain. We arrived at Fintry and met the rather miserable actors and film crew, and the director explained what he wanted. Everybody was cheered up by Hercules, who rose to the occasion with his tricks and pranks in spite of the miserable weather, which he hates.

Then the rain stopped and we were ready to roll. The cameras and lights were set up. Andy was dressed up in a ridiculous gladiator's outfit with a hat with a big red feather in it. The actors all took their seats around the arena, and we were off.

Andy strode into the ring, followed by Hercules, who looked this way and that and didn't look very fierce to me. Then he reared up on his hind legs and went for the red feather. It looked very dramatic as Andy pretended to ward off the savage bear. They wrestled and tussled, and then the scene was over and Andy allowed Hercules to have the feather.

He contentedly rolled over on his back and proceeded to rip the thing to pieces. A plaintive voice cried from the watching crowd, 'Please, someone, rescue my feathers!' But nobody was terribly keen to try. In the end, Andy managed to pry them free with the help of some Polo mint bribes.

The scene had gone so well that it did not require to be shot again. The actors and film crew were very impressed and gave my boys a standing ovation as the rain started again. No mean compliment from professionals – but, then, my men were professionals, too. Everybody dashed back to the buses and caravans to snatch a bite to eat and I asked Andy why he had been so flustered when he had come out of the make-up van at the start of the take.

He said that the two make-up men had fluttered about him like a couple of turtle doves, twittering about his strong muscles, slim hips, and so on, as they fitted him into his costume. The crisis came when they said he would have to wear a little leather loincloth. He put it on but not to their satisfaction. 'You'll have to take off your panties, dear,' they cried. Well, what was a red-blooded Scotsman to do? Andy fled the van. I have never seen him look so bashful, and at the end of the take he flatly refused to go back to the van and I had to take his costume back and recover his clothes.

Another film we did with the BBC was *The Four Seasons*, which was presented by David Bellamy. The series was about the history and development of plants. Apparently, many seeds had come to this country at the end of the Ice Age when Britain was still attached to the continent of Europe, and many had been brought in the coats of animals such as bears that wandered about the land.

They wanted a brief scene to illustrate this and found a

nice location at High Force waterfall in North Yorkshire. Hercules the Stone Age bear was to wander up the stream towards the waterfall and find a salmon on a rock. The camera would watch him as he ate it up.

Andy told the director that Hercules would not eat raw salmon. 'Nonsense,' the director replied, 'bears love salmon, and we have brought a beautiful, fresh twenty-pounder for him.'

Sure enough, up came Hercules, looking every inch the wild bear, found the salmon, sniffed it disdainfully and left it where it was.

This was no good at all. What were they to do? Andy suggested that they leave a few tins of Stone Age John West tinned salmon on the rock. In the end they slit open the salmon's belly and packed it with cooked fish. Up came Hercules, as before, and this time, after he had sniffed the fish, he ripped open its belly and guzzled all the cooked meat inside. Once he had cleaned it out, he tossed away the rest of the fish! I don't know what the experts on bears' diets who were watching the programme must have thought.

By 1980 Hercules was very well known in Scotland from his appearances at numerous events and from our touring around with our film, but as yet he was not very well known in the south, or abroad. It was by chance that he was discovered for the role that would see his photograph appear in every city in the kingdom.

British Airways had embarked on an advertising campaign for their Poundstretcher scheme, which was based on using appropriate animals to appear in the posters. To advertise the cheap fares to South Africa, for example, they used an elephant; for Australia, a kangaroo; and for Canada they needed a bear. The posters would show a fisherman and his son smilingly returning from a successful day on the river, little realising that there was a grizzly bear tiptoeing up behind them.

The South African and Australian projects had been realised without any great difficulty. The Canadian one was a different matter, however. The advertising agency had searched the length and breadth of the USA and Canada to find a bear that could be safely taken under the lights of a photographic studio. Without success.

They were about to abandon the project when they heard that there was a bear in the Highlands of Scotland that might fill the bill.

We were contacted by a photographic studio near Edinburgh and confidently replied that Hercules could do the job.

The session took ten minutes! The photographer was amazed at how relaxed and assured Herc had been. He said it had taken him two days to get the picture he wanted of an elephant's trunk, and five hours to take a suitable picture of the fisherman and his son, which was to be used with Hercules.

This project led directly to the biggest advertising scheme that Herc has been involved in to date: the Kleenex tissues 'Big Softy' campaign.

A couple of months later the photographer who worked with us on the Poundstretcher project was talking to a friend in the same business, and asked what she was involved in at the moment.

'I'm working on this film for Kleenex,' she said, 'which features a lumberjack being wrestled by a bear. Impossible project. You don't happen to know any tame bears who might oblige?' she laughed.

'As a matter of fact I do,' came the reply.

Two days later she and two assistants arrived at Sheriffmuir from London. We had given her details on the telephone and told her that we were sure Hercules could do the job. She wanted to believe us, but it was clear when the southerners arrived that they doubted whether it would be possible.

Often, when it was important for Hercules to give of his best, he would rise to the occasion brilliantly, and so it was that day. He proceeded to charm the pants off the Londoners with his good-natured antics and obvious star quality. The 'Big Softy' was born that day.

Having found a bear, the next thing was to find an actor to play the part of Hank, the lumberjack, who is accosted by the bear in the advertisement. Andy was the obvious person for the part, both because of his relationship with Hercules and because of his physique, but, because of the rules of Equity, the actors' union, the part would have to be auditioned in the usual way.

The part advertised required an actor to be attacked from behind by an almost full-grown, 9-foot-tall, 54-stone grizzly bear. Five brave actors auditioned for the role. Each listened in disbelief as this was outlined to him by Robert, the enthusiastic director, and each then withdrew his application. Andy would have to do the job himself, but to do this he would have to join Equity, usually a very long and difficult business involving having to work in a theatre for a couple of years.

As it turned out, the actors' union couldn't have been more helpful. So long as the proper forms had been filled in and the job duly advertised to their members, they had no objection to Andy's joining, and thus being able to do the job.

We were due to arrive on location very early in the morning, so we drove there in the coach when it was still dark, arriving in time to meet Robert for an early breakfast. The site was in the middle of a large forest in Surrey and it was a tricky job getting the bus down the winding country lanes. Once we arrived, the brightly painted coach looked eerily out of place among the tall trees. Technicians and film crew were arriving all the time – there seemed to be dozens of them in the gloom.

After breakfast we consulted with the wardrobe lady. I was reminded of Andy's previous brush with her profession. Here we immediately ran into difficulties. Although they had brought the biggest woodsman's shirts they could get, none of them were big enough. Indeed, the first one they tried on my big man ripped down a seam as soon as he flexed his muscles. Although he pretended to be annoyed at this, in fact he was secretly proud of the fact that his biceps were substantially bigger than most men's. Here was a real problem: we could not put off the shooting to find a shirt, yet it would look strange if the lumberjack were working naked.

Just then a man who had been watching everything with

keen interest stepped forward and said that he thought he could help. He disappeared for a moment and then returned with the perfect shirt for the job. He said he had been given it in Canada and wouldn't take anything for it.

After Andy's hair had been combed into a new style – he steadfastly refused to be made up – we were ready to go, and walked up a steep hill to where the filming was to be done. Earlier, we had familiarised Hercules with the woods, so he felt quite at home as he walked with the rest of the crew. He seemed to sense that he was in for a bit of fun and the crew, although they had been wary to begin with, soon put their fears behind them. Throughout the rest of the time they spent filming they treated Hercules like a big teddy bear, unperturbed as he walked among them, occasionally bumping into their legs.

'Oh, sorry, Herc,' they would say, carrying on with their business as if it were the most natural thing in the world to have a grizzly bear running around their feet.

CHAPTER 7

BEAR ON THE LOOSE

Fate has a mysterious way of threading itself through every life, and, although we had been planning to take a holiday with Hercules on the Hebridean island of Benbecula for two or three years, we had, for one reason or another, never got around to it.

At the beginning of August 1980 a convenient gap arose in our hectic schedule and we decided that the time for our much-talked-about holiday had arrived. Even so, it wasn't going to be a complete holiday, as we intended to kill two birds with one stone. We would visit my mother's family, who came from the Islands, and do some filming of Hercules for a new Kleenex commercial. Our friends Brian and June Davidson made the trip with us and were looking forward, as we were, to a few days of complete rest.

By the time we arrived on Benbecula we seemed to have put behind us months of feverish activity and, although we had the video to make, we felt more carefree than we had done in years. Perhaps Hercules sensed this. We'll never know, but he entered into a relaxed holiday mood with all his boisterous enthusiasm. No child can have been more thrilled with sea and sand than Hercules was then.

Furiously inquisitive, he would career over the dunes, leaping on the strange mounds of seaweed, desperate to get into the sea and yet uncertain as to what would be there when he finally did so. He had never swum in seawater before and the newfound buoyancy all went to show off his aquatic skills even more than usual. Time and again Hercules and Andy would charge into the sea like a pair of vast water babies, and with each dip Hercules would gain in confidence, swimming with more grace and power, surging ahead as though driven by an expensive outboard motor. Should we have realised then what might happen? We didn't. We just watched, and laughed and felt, as always, slightly awed by the power of this marvellous creature we were blessed with.

It was the third day of our holiday, and we were happier than we had ever been. Andy and Hercules, both impatient to get outside, went down to the sea for a pre-breakfast swim. I stood and lazily watched as the boys scrambled in and out of the water. It was tiring just watching them.

After half an hour Andy shouted, 'I think I'll bring him in now and give him his breakfast. If we stay in any longer, we'll both be growing flippers!' I turned and walked back to the coach to get some beans to entice a reluctant Hercules out of the water, when I heard Andy yell, 'Maggie, Maggie, he's off. He's slipped his rope!' I turned to see Hercules thrusting his way through the water, making for a small island near by.

I froze. Andy and Hercules were now 70 feet apart and the gap was widening. Andy, who was always so confident, so much in control, looked powerless, stunned, riveted in the shallows.

Hercules made the island, shook himself with regal nonchalance, and set off again in a northerly direction.

As luck would have it, Callum Macrae, a local lobster fisherman, and his sons Donald and Duncan came past in their small fishing boat. Andy snapped out of his shocked state and begged a lift to the far shore. The Macraes readily agreed, and I watched the small boat's agonisingly slow progress across the narrows. By this time Hercules had bounded to the top of the island and, without so much as a backward glance, had disappeared from sight.

After what seemed like an eternity, the Macraes' boat landed and Andy sprinted off in hot pursuit. I felt particularly helpless as all I could do was to stand and watch, but I was certain in my mind that the worst that could happen was that the pair of them would be back for a late breakfast or, alternatively, an early lunch.

I waited and waited, pacing up and down the shore. Half an hour passed, forty minutes – and then there was Andy shouting. There was urgency in his voice and no Hercules lolloping by his side. Something was badly wrong.

'He's swimming across to the big island. Get the boat, quick!'

'Oh, Lord!' I blurted, knowing that when we had arrived on North Uist we had left our little boat *Bearpower* in Lochmaddy at the ferry port instead of having her with us in case something awful like this happened.

Almost gabbling with panic, I grabbed Brian and June, and, after I'd promised to explain what had happened en route, we set off at breakneck speed for Lochmaddy. Breakneck speed on the Hebrides, of course, is a different thing altogether from breakneck speed in Los Angeles – or Stirling, for that matter. Part of the charm of the islands is that everything happens infuriatingly slowly. As we drove to Lochmaddy I was inwardly screaming with frustration at the restriction of the single-lane road, punctuated with passing places.

It was almost two hours since we had set off and I could feel a cold sweat developing at the thought of trying to launch the boat with the tide half out. Could we get the boat into the water, and, if we could, would the engine start?

Miraculously we got *Bearpower* into the water and started the engine. From there I steered through the channels, uncertain as to the exact direction we should be heading in, and worried that we would hit one of the many submerged rocks.

After ten minutes we spotted Callum lifting creels on the east side of the big island. As we came alongside I shouted above the sputter of the outboard, 'Andy still hasn't found Hercules – have you seen them?' I must have been a ridiculous sight as I was still wearing only a T-shirt, pink shorts and climbing boots, and Callum, looking like an Old Testament prophet, gave a look that was at once kind and reassuring but also mildly reproving as if to say, 'There's no point in getting panicked, lassie.'

'Don't worry,' he said, 'they're on the island and Duncan is away to help Andy find Hercules. You've to wait here for them.'

I felt reassured at once. It seemed as though I had overreacted, yet somehow I couldn't rid myself of a hundred and one nagging doubts. As we sat bobbing in the swell, scanning the island, I thought, 'What if Hercules is lost – really lost? What if the big soft lump is swept away in one of the fierce currents that surround the islands? What if, through fear and disorientation, he attacks somebody?' Much as we both knew and loved Hercules, we knew him only when he was with us, in a world that revolved around baked beans and grapes, order and warmth. Just how he would react in other circumstances was anyone's guess.

Suddenly, in the distance, a figure appeared. Straining our eyes, we made out Duncan, who was waving frantically and pointing to the northeast end of the island.

'Just follow me and mind you dinna fall,' said Callum, as we brought both boats in to land. We hurriedly secured them and scrambled over the seaweed-covered rocks to the heathery cliff.

Duncan told us he thought that Hercules was still on the island and we all set off, trampling through the heather. Like beaters, we walked in a line, shouting ourselves hoarse, but there was neither movement nor answer.

Nature seemed to be mocking us as we raised our feeble voices in shouts of 'Here, Hercky boy! Herc, Herc, Herc!' – only to have the sounds muted by the vast sky and whipping wind.

My thoughts turned to poor brave Andy, as I watched the columns of grey rainclouds marshal themselves on the northern side of the island. It was getting darker and colder. I knew Andy had lost a shoe in the initial mad scramble and was wearing only a pair of shorts.

Quite clearly we needed more help. It would soon be dark. We needed more eyes. I thought of the army rocket range at Benbecula we had passed the previous evening. Surely they would help? I explained to the others my plan to recruit additional helpers and, as we turned back to the boats, the heavens opened.

Amid gusting winds and torrential rain, we battled our way through by car to the base, which has its own airstrip. We were met, well received, and escorted to the control tower, to see if it would be possible to take up the large blue and red Sea King helicopter that was parked at the side of the runway.

Despite the weather, we were soon airborne. I had never flown in a helicopter before and found myself caught up in the childish thrill of my first flight. When I was securely strapped in and my earphones were buzzing, the helicopter scythed its way through the wind to the part of the island where we thought Hercules might be.

Through the open side door, the view was superb. As we swooped towards the island, I began to feel more relaxed than I had since the moment Hercules had broken free. As the pilot approached the area we had asked him to take us to, we spotted *Bearpower*. The helicopter veered in the direction of the boat, and I noticed the familiar colours of Andy's red and blue tracksuit top that he always stored in the boat. 'Thank God he's got some clothes on at last,' I thought. Feeling sure that he must be going back for Hercules, I agreed with the pilot that it would be best if we returned to base.

We were back on the ground within minutes, and, having thanked everyone, we drove back to Peter's Port, never doubting that Andy would soon be back with Hercules tagging along behind him.

Through the darkness I heard the roar of a speedboat and my heart plummeted because I knew that, if it was Callum himself, the boat would not have been travelling at speed.

Once, when he was with us in *Bearpower*, Callum had admitted that he had never travelled so fast in his life, not even in a car – almost as if to say that God has not intended man to travel at speed. And so I knew that Andy was alone in the boat – because Hercules, try as he might, was far too big to get into it.

Andy threw me a rope to tie her up. I fired a flood of questions at him, only to be met by the untypically flat reply, 'We'll get him in the morning.'

As I walked up the pier, Andy, who usually bounded everywhere, shuffled beside me and told me in a tired hollow voice that he thought Hercules must have gone to sleep somewhere, exhausted after a day of constant running and swimming through the strong currents, some of which run up to nine knots (more than 10mph).

Gradually we pieced together the fragments of the day's chase. Andy had lost all his zest, all his sparkle, and he almost mumbled out the story of how, after swimming the narrow channel, Hercules had crossed the island and then, without a second thought, plunged in and started to swim the three-quarters of a mile through ferocious currents to the larger island of Wiay (pronounced Foo-Yae-EE, from its Gaelic spelling Fuidheigh).

Although in the peak of physical condition, as well as being a strong swimmer, Andy could only weakly watch from the top of the cliff, sure that Hercules would be swept away by the lethal current. His last sight of Hercules had been of his brown head being buffeted by the waves as he had swum towards Wiay.

Now the only possible way for Andy to catch Hercules was to cross over to Wiay by island-hopping, crossing each island on foot and swimming the stretches of water between them. Now that he'd lost his training shoe, his right foot was by now bleeding profusely, but still he kept on running over the harsh heather and swimming the murderous narrows, always just too far behind and yet always convinced that he would round a corner, receive a mighty pat on the shoulder and be set upon by his wrestling partner in a bout of mischievousness.

Hours passed and still he could find no sign of either

Hercules or Duncan, who had come to help him and was scouring other parts of the island.

When they met up with each other in the evening it was Duncan, ironically enough, who had sighted Hercules from the peak of the hill. But, knowing that he could not easily get to Hercules – and that, even if he could, he would probably be unable to control him – he had doubled back to search for us, hoping that Hercules would not move too far away from the spot.

After I had heard the story, and seen how exhausted Andy was and examined the extent of the cuts on his foot, we both agreed that he must rest, and that we would set off again at first light.

We both knew that Hercules would be scared: it was his first night alone since he had come to us. But we also knew that, desperately though we wanted to, we were both too exhausted to continue the hunt, while the islands, hazardous enough by day, would be suicide by night, pocked as they are with bogs and crevasses.

THE SECOND DAY

Friday morning dawned at last to end a lonely night. We had both slept badly, missing desperately that familiar rumbling and snoring from the back of the coach.

We were up at the crack of dawn and Andy and Brian headed straight for Wiay. June and I waited for the soldiers from the base, who had volunteered their help.

The soldiers, sixty in number, arrived at 6.30 a.m. along with the local police and we set off in convoys, each convoy split into two search parties taking a different starting point on the island and working its way inland.

I was with the group that included the very cheerful policeman Sergeant Anderson, a tower of strength, who was to be so kind to us over the coming weeks. Despite my anxiety, I couldn't help smiling at Sergeant Anderson's calls of, 'Here, Hercky boy, here, Herc!' as if he were calling a puppy or coaxing a kitten out of a tree. If Hercules had risen in front of him, to his full 8 feet in height, I'm sure he would have fainted.

We trudged on. My legs were aching from yesterday's exertions, and it always seemed to be a struggle to get through the dense heather. The fact that I was carrying Andy's bag filled with beans and meat didn't make my life any easier. I was constantly slipping and stumbling like a Saturday-night drunk.

As the day wore on, and the crackling reports on the soldiers' walkie-talkies made it apparent that the other groups were having as little success as we were, I began to cry inwardly from exhaustion and fear.

I just couldn't understand it. It was so unlike our boy. He was always rushing to and fro in his eagerness to find out what was over the next hill.

'Oh, please, God where are they?' I prayed, as my eyes filled with tears. Then I spotted Andy. Someone was running towards him. My heart thumped, and I rushed forward – I knew they had found him. 'Have you seen him?' I shouted. 'They've found some prints over there,' Andy said, pointing to the north.

We all trudged behind the two soldiers who had seen his prints. 'If his prints are there, surely he can't be too far away,' I said. 'Keep your fingers crossed, babe,' said Andy, who seemed close to tears himself.

The sun was blazing down and I was relieved of my burden of beans and meat. We reached the peaty patch where the soldiers had found the two paw prints. Having closely examined them, Andy said, 'Well, that proves he's been here.' But I think we all doubted what we saw. After almost two days of searching we had come across only two prints, no more, because the peat patch was small and surrounded on all sides by heather. The two big paw marks seemed to start and end from nowhere, just as though Hercules had been whisked away into thin air.

We spread out and searched all around the area, but no other prints were found, the only movements coming from a group of puzzled sheep who looked surprised to see their sunny day disturbed.

In this barren wilderness of peat bogs and heather searching seemed futile. Heather, that simple hardy plant much loved by tourists, who stick it in tweed caps and car radiators, was a stubborn foe that seemed to blur the vision in a mist of browns and purples – disguising valleys and hills alike.

We had all been on the island for almost seven hours. The further we went, the greater our task seemed to be. Knowing that we could not ask again for the Royal Navy Sea King helicopter from the base, as it was needed for secret testing in the North Sea, I suggested to Andy that we hire a civilian one. He agreed, but said that he would stay on the island to continue searching on foot.

It was 2 p.m., and for the second time in two days I was driven to the airstrip at Benbecula. Once there, we were told that it would take a helicopter we had managed to hire an hour and a half to arrive from Glasgow.

I couldn't find the energy to speak. I sat waiting, staring blankly ahead of me, trying to keep the fears back, and saying my private prayers in the hope that God would let us find our boy, my baby.

The control tower filled with people: police, press, army and our trusted old friend Eddie Orbell from the wildlife park at Kingussie, where Hercules was born. I saw the sympathetic look in Eddie's eyes as he said in his soft southern accent, 'We'll get him for you, Maggie. He's out there somewhere.' And a lump came into my throat. I had to swallow hard and grit my teeth to stop myself crying.

Minutes were like hours. I kept my eyes averted from everyone, knowing that I had to keep calm, knowing I had to stop my boiling emotions from spilling over, as I had to try to be alert in order to be able to go up in the helicopter and try to spot Hercules.

Eventually, the helicopter [so much smaller than the big robust one I had first taken to the air with] landed outside the control tower. After a few minutes' delay for a fuel check, I was aboard, strapping myself in and securing the mike. The rotor blades roared above us, and we were airborne.

We swept over Wiay, back and forth, back and forth, methodically combing the island, section by section, down to only a matter of feet above the ground if we saw something we thought was moving or might possibly be Hercules.

My head ached with the buzz of the headphone and I thought my eyeballs would burst out of their sockets with the strain of looking so hard.

We had four pairs of eyes: my own, the pilot's and our faithful friends Brian's and June's. But still we could see nothing, except sheep that remained calm despite the roar of the helicopter. Hercules could not be seen.

'I think we should try the mainland of Benbecula itself now,' I told the pilot. 'He may've swum back over there.'

We could fly even lower over the ground on the flat stretches of Benbecula, ut our search of the main island proved just as fruitless as our search of Wiay. As we swept over the bogs and neatly stacked piles of peat, the crofters would wave as if to wish us well. All the islanders seemed to know what was happening, as nothing remains a secret in the Hebrides for long.

When we returned to the airport we were greeted by official cars and what seemed like hundreds of stern, uniformed men. Perhaps it was my imagination but these grim-faced men seemed just as worried as we were, already bound up in our agonising adventure, and no doubt worrying whether Hercules would lay waste to the islands.

I stepped from the helicopter shaking my head in disbelief. 'There's no sign of him at all. If he'd been moving, we would have seen him,' I said. Andy looked at me, his face drawn with worry. It was as if we were both caught in an unending nightmare, with nothing seeming to be as it should have been. Everyone surrounding us seemed remote; we were floating, totally lost. Andy put his big strong arms around my shoulder and said, 'He must still be on the island; we just haven't looked in the right place, that's all.' It was finally all too much for me and I openly wept like a baby.

We called off the search for that day and went back to the coach to eat and sleep, determined to search Wiay again in the morning. This time we would use more soldiers and tracker dogs brought over from Skye. Surely we would find him tomorrow.

THE THIRD DAY

After another night, when we both seemed to be more often awake than asleep, we started our search again. We tried to give each other new hope, saying how the tracker dogs must be able to help, and how Hercules must by now be ravenously hungry and on the lookout for food, which would surely make him easier to find.

But we were both nagged by awful unspoken doubts, not wanting to depress each other even further. We both knew that Hercules had not run away from us, but, in playing a game and being thrilled with the newfound buoyancy of the sea, he had swum too far. Now he was lost and frightened and, in attempting to get back to us, he may actually be going further away.

Daylight brings comfort in the same strange way as darkness turns the mind to imagining the blacker side of things, and so we did not set out in an entirely hopeless state.

In due course the army arrived in a convoy of buses and

Land Rovers. The tracker dogs were not far behind them. The three dogs were unloaded from blue vans by their handlers.

It was not long until we were on Wiay again and we once more divided into groups. It surprised me that the handlers did not want any piece of clothing with Hercules's scent on it – but they assured me that the dogs would pick up any strange smell. I crossed my fingers and nodded, presuming my preconceptions about tracker dogs to be wrong, but silently doubting that the dogs could pick up Hercules's subtle, almost nonexistent woody scent.

I stayed with the middle group and a black Alsatian, who looked keen to start. Together with a soldier with a walkie-talkie connected to base, we set off into the wind.

Although I was once again carrying my bag of food, ready to run to the scene at the first hint of a sighting, walking was much easier that day, as we kept to the higher ground, avoiding the peat marshes.

The dogs stayed out in front so that any strange scent might not be confused with our own. We tried to keep them in view at all times, but this proved impossible. The lie of the land was such that dogs and handlers were constantly disappearing from view.

My eyes were by now becoming accustomed to the constant, slow, sweeping searches I carried out through the high-powered binoculars. I took in every dark object and concentrated hard on it in order to identify exactly what it was.

We started our search on the south side of the island and

worked our way northwards to where Duncan had last sighted him, on the first day.

When we had been walking for two or three hours, I heard a shout and, turning, saw that the soldier to my right had sunk to his waist in the bog. He was sinking fast and each movement he tried to make only took him deeper. I realised that I had to act quickly and removed my jacket. Edging towards the boggy patch, I threw the sleeve to him. He caught it and within a minute I had managed to work him free. He was visibly shaken, and, as he was wiping himself down, said, 'I hope Hercules didn't do what I did.'

'I hope not,' I replied, not wanting to hurt the soldier's pride by telling him that Hercules was far too sensible and too cautious to go blundering into a bog. Hercules would never normally tread on anything if he suspected the ground might give way. He might come to the edge of a bog, but his quick mind and strong instinct for self-preservation would usually prevent him from going any further, and he would tread warily until he had found a better route to take.

When we finally climbed to the top of the highest peak on Wiay we could watch the dogs on both sides of us and had a much better idea of what was happening. I caught sight of Andy at the east side of the island and saw him drop disconsolately to the ground. I wished then that he had been up on top of the hill with me, to offer me comfort and be comforted in return. The dogs had neither seen nor smelled anything unusual and after another hour I went over to join Andy to see if he had found any traces of our lost boy.

I could see the disappointment written over his broad,

suntanned face. He and Archie – a taxi driver who had joined our band of helpers – had found another couple of footprints but nothing else. Once again the prints had disappeared into thin air, as though someone were playing a cruel game with us, building up our hopes only to dash them again.

We decided to search in the direction the footprints were leading, so we made for the northeast of the island, searching every crack as we went in the hope of finding more prints or some – any – kind of lead.

The rest of the soldiers had by now started to head southwards, and would be coming to the end of their search. It seemed that we were all looking in completely the wrong places, since there were any number of small islands he could have swum to in his panic.

For the third day we had to admit defeat. My legs felt as if I would never walk again and, although Andy's physical strength had not deserted him, he was utterly frustrated mentally. If the islands themselves knew where Hercules was hiding, they were not willing to yield their secrets.

Back at Peter's Port, we were met by hordes of reporters and photographers, all anxious to learn if we had any news. But I had nothing to say – I could only think of myself and could not find a single word to express how I felt. The day seemed a dismal repetition of the one before and the day before that. Andy tried to put a brave face on it, saying, 'He's out there watching us all. He's probably sitting behind a rock, feet up, thoroughly enjoying his holiday.' His reply brought a chorus of laughter amid the gloom. Perhaps the press could not notice, as I could, how much Andy's voice was tingling with sadness, and that, even though he was hiding his anguish well, it would not take much to bring my mighty man to his knees.

I sat in a corner of the coach, my eyes sore and puffy, staring into space. Of course, I knew that everyone meant well and I could see the affection and concern they felt for Hercules, but that did not ease the pain.

Later that night Andy Higgins of the *Daily Mail* came to the coach and with tears in his eyes said, 'I would willingly give a million pounds and give up my job if I could help you get Hercules back. I'm so sorry.'

'If only he were here to see how much everybody loves him,' I thought, and dropped my head into my hands, trying to hide my tears.

After everyone had gone and we were alone again, Andy sat looking longingly at the island, as if, by his staring long enough and hard enough, Hercules would simply appear and the nightmare would be over.

He turned to me, his eyes looking tired and bloodshot. 'They think he's drowned, don't they?' I nodded. He turned away and I saw his shoulders heave. The dam had burst and his tears flowed, but even in front of me, he was still trying to hide them. I knew only too well how he felt and wanted to tell him to let it all out, but the words seemed to stick in my throat. He got up and walked down to the end of the pier. I could only stare hopelessly at his broad back and pray once more that this nightmare would end.

We ate some supper that night, not from hunger, but from

the realisation that we had to maintain our strength to be able to keep searching. The food went down, but tasted of nothing. That night was the worst yet. Our nightmare was becoming a reality: it was happening, and the empty room at the back of the coach was the glaring proof of it all.

Peace would not come that night, even though every one of my muscles ached with tiredness. Once again, I lay awake staring at the sky, trying to doze intermittently, only to wake once more.

Andy had withdrawn into himself. The only thing in his life that he felt no embarrassment over demonstrating his love for had vanished. I awoke in a sweat to find him turned away from me, his body racked with sobs. In the darkness his tears had found an outlet. I turned and bit the pillow as I tried to muffle the sound of my own sobs, thinking how two people normally so close suddenly, through necessity, can shut each other out, by trying not to make the other any more unhappy through their own sadness.

THE FOURTH DAY

The fourth day dawned wild and blustery, the rain beating a tattoo on the roof of the coach. Until now the weather, with the exception of the wind and rain on the first day, had been fair – and my thoughts turned to Hercules and to how he hated the rain, preferring in bad weather to stay lying in his den listening to music that filtered through from the kitchen or the bar, and only venturing out to see if the day looked like brightening up.

The previous evening Duncan had told us, not meaning to

worry us further but to ensure that the fullest possible search was made, that there were twelve large hidden crevasses on the island of Wiay. These were not easy to find, and known only to the local shepherds and fishermen. They were covered by a thick layer of heather, and hence invisible to the eye, but once the heather was parted, or any real pressure was placed on it, the ground fell away in a sheer drop some 150 feet to the sea below. He thought it best that we checked these crevasses to see if Hercules had fallen into one of them.

Although we knew Hercules to be cautious, we realised that there was the chance of his having made some ghastly mistake, and so we resolved to spend the day checking the crevasses, and rechecking the small lochs on the centre of the island. We could not rule out any possibility – and we were haunted by the thought that Hercules might be lying suffering at the bottom of a gully or crevasse.

The day started along the now familiar lines. Once we had split into groups, we began to comb the island again.

That day I was walking with an islander called Davie Shepherd, who was always ready with a smile and encourage-ment, and would produce endless sweets from a large bag he carried with him. Davie was full of theories as to where Hercules could be and we tried them one by one, finishing with the crevasses, which was no easy task. After that we had exhausted even his fertile imagination.

We went on to search all the tiny islands surrounding Wiay. Each one, small though it might be, had to be thoroughly investigated, for we were determined to leave no stone unturned.

During the afternoon the seas mounted, and we had to stick close to the coast. As we made our way back to Peter's Port, the fishermen who were with us started to talk of the Minch, the formidable stretch of water between the Inner and Outer Hebrides, famed for being one of the most unpredictable in the British Isles. They talked of how the treacherous currents had claimed many fishing boats, and, though they did not say so, it was clear they felt that Hercules might have made for the only visible land mass – Skye on the other side of the Minch.

On a clear day, such as it had been when Hercules first disappeared, the cliffs of Skye were just visible on the horizon. My secret feeling was that he had far too much common sense to think he could swim that far. I just couldn't believe he had set off into the wild blue yonder.

In the four years since we had brought Hercules home from the Wildlife Park at Kingussie we had time and again marvelled at his common sense. Once, when we were at Loch Earn and Hercules was out swimming with us, he started to swim across the loch. When he had gone almost a third of a mile he started back, seeming to realise that he might not get to the other side safely. Andy and I had always remarked to each other, like two proud parents, that, where everything else would perish, Hercules would survive.

Surely he could not have lost all his common sense in a few days, and thrown his life away without a thought, could he? No, not my Hercules! With this thought, which Andy, of course, shared, we decided that, somewhere, Herc was still alive – the big question was: where?

That night we decided, having asked our friends in the press to publicise it for us, that we would offer a reward of a thousand pounds to the first person who sighted Hercules, on the understanding that the sighting must lead to his recapture.

THE FIFTH DAY

For the first time since we lost Hercules, I had a decent night's sleep. Whether or not it was through sheer fatigue I didn't know, but I woke only once on that windy night, and snuggled into Andy, who was asleep like a log beside me.

The local gamekeepers had sent word to us the previous evening that they would like to try to help us find Hercules. They offered not only their own services but also those of their dogs, and we were only too glad to accept their help. Grateful though we were, the tracker dogs had been no use, but the gun dogs were used to driving into deep heather to retrieve game, and so they might be of real help in raising a sleeping Hercules. The heather was so dense that it would be possible to pass within feet of him and miss him, since his coat would blend perfectly with the natural surroundings – just as nature intended.

True, it was a slim chance that Hercules would be sleeping in the wild during the day, but it was another possibility that we could not overlook, since the freak events of the past few days may have triggered off his hibernation cycle.

In the wild, hibernation is normally a gradual process that happens to bears during the late autumn months, when food begins to run short and the weather is deteriorating. The bear's body then produces a drug that enters the bloodstream and it begins sleeping for increasingly long periods of time until full hibernation is reached.

It was only late August and still relatively warm in the Hebrides, and so it was unlikely that Hercules would have drifted into this state, but perhaps hunger and the shock of being lost had made him hide and, in turn, sleep.

There was no food on the islands, other than shellfish on the shore and sheep. Although Hercules ate only cooked food, the possibility that he might try to kill a sheep had, of course, entered our heads, but that would be foreign to his whole upbringing. If he was in the wild long enough, we had no doubt that he would learn to kill – that is, if he didn't starve to death first – but, as it was, he was only used to running in the field with the sheep at home. There he had caught them only to get a sniff of them. Then he had let them run away, and the worst they had suffered was a slight shock.

Hercules always went out of his way not to hurt anything. Even the month-old kitten he had trapped under his massive paws received no more than a loving lick from the gentle giant.

When we started out on the day's search I was aching all over, stiff with the last few days' exercise as well as suffering a lot of pain from a back injury I had sustained falling from a horse earlier in the summer.

The tweed-clad keepers were prompt, and their dogs, which at first I thought looked too old for a full day's work, were more than up to the job. They were eager and obedient, diving into the undergrowth and popping up every now and then as if to make sure that they were keeping their masters happy.

Andy and I watched from a few paces behind, and walked silently for most of the day, ever hopeful that the enthusiastic retrievers would raise Hercules from his slumber.

Yet again the island yielded nothing and, as we took the now familiar way back to the boat, the awful doubts began to set in again.

We had now eliminated all the obvious and not so obvious hiding places, had covered in one way or another every nook and cranny of Wiay, and we were still without a single clue, other than the two sets of isolated footprints.

Somehow, Andy was managing to put on a brave face for all the well-wishers who continually appeared in Peter's Port to show their concern and offer suggestions as to where Hercules might be.

Every day the papers were full of news. The cartoons of Hercules drinking with his new Highland neighbours would have been funny, but for the seriousness of the whole situation. Headlines reading HERCULES BEATS THE ARMY or HERCULES TAKES A BREAK FROM STARDOM stared out of practically every paper in the country, with even *The Sunday Times* giving him front-page billing.

'If only he were here to see it,' I sighed, picturing his great, big, gentle head and soft brown eyes.

THE SIXTH DAY

Tuesday, the sixth day since Hercules had gone missing, arrived. The weather continued to be bad and the spring tides were running. Bankrupt of ideas, we decided that Andy should visit South Uist, as it was just conceivable that Hercules might have reached there by crossing the flats at low tide and swimming where it was necessary.

It was agreed that I should stay at the coach in case Hercules should be spotted, and, desperate though I was to find him, I welcomed the opportunity to rest.

There was not a trace of Hercules on South Uist, and it was totally unrealistic to imagine we had a hope of finding him should he be there, unless he was accidentally sighted or we had several thousand men to search it from top to bottom. The mountains were steep and pitted with small caves and gullies, a climbers' paradise but a searchers' nightmare.

Our hopes were wearing very thin. We felt that all we could do now was to sit and wait for someone to spot our boy. It was stalemate. Our conversations were becoming less and less frequent and more stilted, as we each brooded over our unspoken thoughts and fears.

Just as we had reached the point when our morale was at breaking point, we received good news. A pilot from Stornoway on the Isle of Lewis contacted us to say that he would fly us over the islands.

It was just what we needed. In a light plane we could scan the difficult terrain much more thoroughly than on foot, and I rang him that evening to accept his kind offer. He agreed to fly down the next morning if the weather was suitable. Once again, the pain in my heart seemed to ease a little, with renewed hope for tomorrow.

THE SEVENTH DAY

The next day I was eager to be off as soon as possible. Brian and June, who had come only to make a video of Hercules and who had been unwittingly caught up in the whole drama, were going home. Not driven with the same compulsion as we were, nor as physically fit, they were completely exhausted. The daily searching had punished us all, and, as they struggled to secure the towbar of the caravan to the ball coupling on their car, they looked desperate to get away from the intricate nightmare Andy and I were plunged into. We would miss them because they had been with us from the very start.

However, Andy and I could not get away from our nightmare so easily. My mind kept saying over and over again, 'If only we had gone somewhere else, if only . . .' But we couldn't leave, we had to go on.

Brian was going to give me a lift to the airport, and, as I climbed into his car, binoculars in hand, Andy shouted, 'I'm going over to Wiay again. I've a funny feeling that he's still there. I'll see you when you get back.' Confusion was written all over his weary unshaven face. He just couldn't take it all in. Refusing to admit to the full reality of Hercules's disappearance seemed to be Andy's passport to sanity in a world turned upside down.

Once at the airport and having said goodbye to Brian and June, I telephoned the pilot, Bob Ford-Sagers. He said that the conditions were too hazy, but that if I could wait at the airport he would phone back as soon as he felt visibility was improving. Of course, I agreed, and waited six hours, drinking endless cups of tea and coffee.

The day did not clear up, and eventually Morag, an assistant to the controller, called a taxi for me. Once again I felt completely useless, a pawn in a game over which nobody – I least of all – had any control.

When I got back to Peter's Port I was confronted with a rare sight – Andy was smiling. My heart leapt and I felt my stomach churn. At last, it must be good news.

As I stepped out of the car, Andy beamed at me and said, 'I found his collar. I knew he'd been to the island for a while – I just knew it. Quick, get the kettle on and we'll have a cup of tea – he's over there somewhere sleeping. I just know it.'

This was the old Andy I had almost forgotten, smiling and jabbering away nineteen (at least) to the dozen. It was the quickest cup of tea I've ever had – it went down in seconds – and once again we were off.

Wiay seemed to hold the key to the mystery. Perhaps the island was ready to give up her secret, because today, as we made the crossing, even the sea seemed friendlier, the lapping of the waves gentler.

I ran and half walked to keep up with Andy, laughing happily at the thought of all three of us reunited, being able to return together to our familiar routine at Sheriffmuir.

We reached the place where Andy had found Hercules's collar, and it gave a sudden injection of hope. We had been searching the island for a week and had passed the spot at least a hundred times.

Standing on the path looking downwards towards a small loch, I noticed that the heather and ferns at the very edge of the water were flattened, as if they had been trodden on. I slid down the banking and landed in a perfect den. It was completely hidden, commanded a panoramic view, and was embedded in the very side of the loch at water level, camouflaged by an overhanging roof of peat and ferns. The sides were scooped out to give it walls, and a layer of soil and ferns at least 6 inches deep made a comfortable mattress. To the front was a small row of slim-stemmed rowan trees, which prevented anyone from looking into the den, but allowed the inhabitant a perfect view. It was definitely Hercules's – it carried all his trademarks.

'He must have spent at least one night here, maybe more,' I said excitedly, delighted with my find.

'I'm sure he's on this island somewhere,' Andy kept repeating, as we set off again to look at all the really deep lochs. We had searched them all before, but some were so steeply banked that we had not gone right down to the water's edge. On this occasion we intended to do a much more thorough job.

Many of the lochs were so steep that Andy had to swim round them, while I scrambled along the sides, the bag of food cutting into my shoulders and all the while being mercilessly bitten by the midges that abounded in the clammy heat of the loch sides.

I watched Andy swimming below me, peering into every

Andy and Herc
reunited.

"Hercule est un vrai bébé !"

Quand nous avons adopté Hercule, il n'avait que quelques mois. Naturellement, il n'existait aucun manuel intitulé "Comment élever un ours". Alors, nous nous sommes fiés à notre instinct et nous lui avons prodigué tout notre amour. Il est entouré de gentillesse et ne sait donc pas ce qu'est la méchanceté. Il n'y a que lorsque je lui apporte son repas en retard qu'il grogne "m'man !" raconte Maggie Robin.

Left: A tender moment.

Right: The big fellow in the middle: that's me!
(*Sunday People*)

Left: Hercules accompanies Maggie and tries his hand at show jumping. (*Leslie Lane, AIIP*)

Above. While Andy drives, me and mum are caught kissing again . . .

Right: A very sloppy kiss . . .   (*Sunday Mirror*)

Left: She's my mum!

Above left: Love this white stuff!

Above right: It's snow time!

Below: A snowy day in the hills with Hercules and Sheriffmuir. (*Leslie Lane, AIIP*)

Right: Where are we going this time?

(*Glasgow Herald*)

Left: American idyll.

Right: It's a bear's life.

Above: TV show host Merv Griffin meets Hercules in Los Angeles.

Below: Our American adventure.

Above: The UCLA Bruins introduce Hercules as their mascot in Los Angeles.

Below: California here we come.   (*Scottish Daily Record*)

Right: Happy together.

Left: Trusted and trusting companions.

Right: We three.
(*Sunday People*)

ledge, missing nothing, leaving nothing to chance. We managed to thoroughly search four large lochs and several small ones that afternoon, before the intense cold of the dark peaty water forced Andy to retire for the day, his body a kaleidoscope of blue, purple and white blotches. Tomorrow, we would return, equipped with wetsuits.

THE EIGHTH DAY

I woke early with the coach being buffeted by a strong wind, and, turning to look at the sleeping Andy, wondered how long his strength could last. Letting him go on sleeping, I thought of the events of the last cruel week, and wondered what the outcome would be.

I still could not really believe Hercules had gone, and, looking at his empty den at the back of the bus, I thought of him looking at me, scolding me for not having got out of bed sooner to make his normal gallon of tea.

Andy stirred, and turned towards me, saying nothing, but knowing immediately how I was feeling. Each day we woke in hope, and when darkness fell we were left alone with our despair and frustration. As we constantly tried to put ourselves in Hercules's position, imagining what he would do, we knew that at best we were only wildly guessing. Of course, our doubts as to whether Hercules was still alive had grown, but still we stubbornly refused to accept even the possibility.

I made a good hearty breakfast for us that day, knowing that, unless the weather improved drastically, the plane would be unable to make the crossing from Stornoway, because of this we realized we would have to continue our search of the lochs without it and hope that at some point it could get to us.

Both wearing wetsuits, I combed the higher edges of the loch sides while Andy continued his marathon swims around the lochs.

The day began to brighten up, and my wetsuit, which had been a blessing when we started out in the cold wet morning, became a curse.

Even after I had unzipped the jacket the heat was unbearable. My legs and back were excruciatingly painful, and, after I had stumbled over the heather for the umpteenth time, tears of rage, frustration and utter disappointment filled my eyes. As I lay sobbing, I realised that I just could not go on, and passed the point of no return. Andy knelt down beside me and took me in his arms.

'I think we'll go back now. I'll come back later on. There are only two more lochs to do.' I knew he was trying to spare my feelings and let me off the hook, so I got up and stumbled down the hill with him.

As we were mooring the boat back at Peter's Port we heard a buzzing overhead and looked up to see a small yellow and white plane circling over the island. Bob had managed to fly down after all.

We watched for a while and then walked back to the coach. There we learned that Archie the taxi driver had twice come down to the port trying to contact us, and, failing to do so, had gone up in the plane with Bob to act as the second pair of eyes.

I flopped into one of the chairs on the coach and had just closed my eyes for a second, when Andy put his hand on my shoulder and said, 'Maggie, I think you should go to the airport. There's no sense in them flying over the island any more, so get the control tower to tell Bob to start searching the mainland.'

There now seemed little real hope that we would ever find Hercules. Andy was by now at the lowest I had ever known him. Like a drowning man clinging to wreckage, he refused to let go of the idea that Hercules was still alive. He had done everything humanly possible, had driven himself beyond his physical limits and further. He could find nothing to say, nothing to suggest, but he was staying – by God he was – until he knew either way.

Words just seemed to make it worse. I spent hours trying to reason with him that he had done all he could, and finally I persuaded him to fly home with me. He could leave the coach with my uncle, Archie, and if Hercules was sighted we could be back up on the island within an hour and a half.

It was while we were packing that the awful finality of what we were doing began to sink in: we were leaving without Hercules. We had one last farewell to make at my uncle's house on Grimsay – and it was there that fate chose to take another cruel turn.

When we arrived at my uncle's house, my aunt, Effie, a primary-school teacher, said that she had heard an odd story at school that day. On arriving at school the children had been full of gossip about the carcass of a sheep being stolen.

I saw Andy's face light up as he waited eagerly to hear the rest of the story.

Effie went on to tell us that seemingly, in a stretch of land called Eochar on the island of South Uist, a crofter had had his barn door broken in, a sheep carcass torn in two, and half of it stolen. It sounded just the sort of thing Hercules might do – especially if, as he must have been, ravenously hungry.

On hearing the news Andy immediately asked Uncle Archie to telephone around to see if there was any truth in the story. After a few phone calls we learned that, yes, it was true.

Archie drove us hastily to Eochar, to the rather rundown croft of a Mr McQueen, but had warned us on the way not to expect too much, for we were obviously eager to grasp at any new leads offered.

We arrived at the house and were met by two young men, who showed us the shed where the carcass had been hanging. The door was indeed off its hinges.

Andy and I looked at each other, shaking our heads and not wanting to expect too much, but, as always, any small spark quickly rekindled the fires of hope inside us.

The shed was old and had a thatched roof. We had a good look inside and tried to visualise what Hercules would have done in the situation. We both agreed, laughing, that he would have been extremely sneaky, practically tiptoeing out of the shed, having first peeped round the corners to make sure the coast was clear.

Andy told the young men that he would have to inform the police and get the search going again. The dark-headed one, who slouched with his hands in his pockets, said, keeping his eyes firmly fixed on the floor, 'You'll have to tell the old man first.'

'Where is he?' asked Andy, eager to get going.

'He'll be down in Creagorry,' said the spokesman, his eyes still averted. 'We'll get him for you, just wait here.' And the pair walked away, looking unhappy about the whole affair.

After half an hour there was still no sign of the old man. We were thinking perhaps the bird had flown the coop.

At last a car drew up and what was clearly 'the old man' got out. 'Hello there,' said Andy. 'Can we talk about the missing carcass?'

'Yes, but if the police come I'll say that I knocked the door down myself. You see, the boys might get into trouble for having the carcass hanging in the shed in the first place.'

'That's fine with me,' said Andy, interested only in learning anything he could tell us about Hercules.

'The old man' told us how he had never seen anything like it in his life, and he drew a diagram on the steamed-up car window of how he had discovered the carcass torn in two.

'I'm not saying it was your bear, mind,' he said, 'but it would take a phenomenal strength to do it – it couldn't have been a dog, and I don't want to tell you no lies but I've never seen nothing like it.'

He sat silently smiling, waiting for an answer.

'Did you see any unusual paw marks?' Andy said, looking him straight in the eye. The old man pushed his cap further up on his head, and scratched his temple with a nicotine-stained finger.

'Well, there may have been, and there may not have been,' Mr McQueen replied enigmatically. 'What I saw,' he continued, 'was more a sort of group of wee circles, each about an inch and a half in diameter like paw prints.

And, to our delight, they resembled Hercules's.

'Now, I'm telling you no lies,' he said, looking sternly at us both. 'That's what I saw.'

Andy and I were convinced, and, although the old man looked a bit of a wag, we believed him. It all seemed to fit.

Once back at my uncle's house we telephoned the police. Instead of receiving the news enthusiastically they were extremely sceptical as to the validity of the story, but they said they would look into the matter just the same.

Our plans to go home the next day were put to one side, as we promised each other that, if it had been Hercules who had taken the carcass, we would search the area until we found him.

Having been in the depths of depression only six hours earlier, we went to bed that night more cheerful than at any time since Hercules had gone missing and, after eating a delicious supper cooked by Aunt Effie, we were asleep in seconds.

I awoke next morning with Andy's arms around me. He kissed me and said, 'Well, babe, let's hope things look as promising this morning as they did last night.' I nodded, and silently prayed that he was right.

I telephoned the police station straight after breakfast and asked to speak to Sergeant Anderson. I was told that he had been out at Eochar since the early morning and I was given a number there. My lips were dry with anticipation as I dialled the number.

'Hello, may I speak to Sergeant Anderson, please?' I said. 'Yes. Just one moment,' came a voice from the other end. Sergeant Anderson came to the phone.

'It's Maggie Robin, Sergeant,' I began. 'What do you think? It's just like Hercules would do, isn't it?' I had no doubt that he would agree and I could visualise telephoning the army to tell them that the search could be resumed on the strength of the new evidence. His answer stunned me.

'No, Maggie, I'm afraid not. Of course I don't know the bear as well as you, but we have thoroughly searched the area and can't find any evidence of him having been there. I'm very sorry. I know how disappointed you must be.'

'What about the door, the carcass?' I asked. 'I know it's hard, Maggie, but, between you and me, we are ninety per cent certain it was a human animal that broke the door and stole the carcass, if you know what I mean.'

I couldn't believe what he was saying, nor believe that all our rekindled hope could vanish in a few seconds. Despite Sergeant Anderson's devastating news, we decided that we should search the area in case the police had missed something. Somehow, we dragged ourselves through the next two days, as we scoured the beaches and dunes, oblivious of the beautiful scenery, and intent only on finding some clue that would say our boy was still alive.

It was late on that bleak Wednesday evening that we finally made the decision to go home. We had not so much run out of places to look but, in the vastness of the desolate stretches of land, we did not know where to start. It would take years to search every peaty bog and, even then, who could be sure that we would cover the spot where our boy was lying?

We had to admit defeat, at least for the time being. Nature had pitted her wits against us and had been returned the victor. A mighty adversary indeed.

All the goodbyes had been said, all the thank-yous had been given. Amid the nightmare we had found friendship and comradeship that came only from the sincerity of the heart. The islanders had taken us into their lives and shown us kindness that could not be measured in depth, and a kinship that grew from the fact that they lived their lives needing each other. Nothing was asked in return.

We had come to the islands with our lives full, a happy threesome, delighting in the pleasure we found in each other's company, but now the vital link was missing. We had lost our boy. Those cheeky eyes that saw all, the bright mind that missed nothing, it was all gone.

CHAPTER 8

HOME AT LAST

On the fourteen-hour journey home we spoke only a few words to each other. In Andy's haggard face I saw the reflection of my own sorrow, coupled with a look of total defeat. I knew that, when we reached the brow of the hill, just before the white walls of the Inn came into view, I would not awake to find that it had all been a dream, and the sight of those familiar surroundings would stab home the enormity of our loss.

As I watched Andy drive the coach back home over the last few miles, I remembered how shocked he had been when, in the early stages of the coach's assembly, someone had inadvertently asked where Herc's door would be. 'Why, he'll use the same door as Maggie and I,' he answered sharply. 'He'll use the front door. It's only an animal that uses a separate door.' It summed up Andy's views on Herc exactly.

As the Inn came into view I felt nothing. Not for a moment did I feel the usual pleasure at coming home to the place I loved. I didn't want to speak to anyone and dreaded the moment when I would have to answer a question from a customer or member of staff.

Margaret, who helped me with my horses, was the first to meet us, and clearly felt awkward, not knowing what to say. Seeing that we did not want to talk, she kept her greeting brief and we gladly made our way to the privacy of our own flat.

The empty rooms were lonely and silent. The walls, covered with photographs and pictures of Hercules, recalled the happy times before we left. Idle chatter from the bar drifted up through the floor, and I sat lost in my thoughts, waiting aimlessly for the barman to come up and say, 'That's it for the night.' And then I could go and lose myself in sleep.

I realised from the first moment on the first day back that Andy could not accept what fate had dealt him. Always grimly determined, especially when the odds were stacked against him, he refused to give up. 'He's still alive, Maggie,' he murmured to me in bed that first morning. 'Somewhere out there in all the wind and rain he's waiting, wondering where his dad is. I've got to go back; I've got to be there, just in case.'

It's strange how a single night can make all the difference, and a new day bring fresh hope to lean upon. 'What can I say?' I thought. 'How can I, knowing that his heart is breaking,

dash even the slightest hope, even if I know that there is none?'
I could see no happy ending, but what could be worse than
the ending we already had? And so we prepared for Andy to
go back, if only just to be near the scene.

Andy was smiling again as we loaded up his pickup truck
with provisions for him and some of Hercules's favourite
food. Always the optimist, he believed then, as he believes
now, that dreams come true if you believe in them strongly
enough. But I could no longer share his simple faith and, as
each day passed with no sign of Hercules, I could only marvel
at how, when Andy rang to say all his efforts had been useless,
he managed to keep any hope alive, for he would end the
conversation by saying, 'Perhaps tomorrow, Maggie.'

I felt completely useless sitting at home waiting for news.
I could not even ride to take my mind off worrying as I
was hardly able to walk because of a twist at the base of my
spine. The days seemed utterly bleak, and, as the osteopath
worked hard trying to get my back into shape, I tried to plan
for the future. Our whole lives were built around Hercules,
and I feared the strain it would put on us, having to adapt to
life without him.

On the eighth day after we had come home I was woken
by the telephone ringing. I glanced at my watch and saw it
was 7.45 a.m., and, just as I was about to get up to answer it,
I realised that my younger brother Alastair, who, sporting a
broken leg from a rugby accident, had been looking after the
Inn in our absence and had stayed on to keep me company,
had already picked up the phone. I heard the click of the
receiver as it was quickly replaced.

Rain was lashing against my bedroom window and, having no good reason to get up, I turned over and went back to sleep, but ten minutes later the telephone rang again. Two calls this early in the morning must mean something, but what? I was too scared even to hazard a guess and, despite my bad back, I leapt out of bed and rushed to the phone in the next room.

I felt my adrenalin surging as I picked up the phone and listened to the voice at the other end of the line. It was Radio Scotland ringing to ask, 'Is it true that Hercules has been spotted?'

'I don't know,' I spluttered, not daring to hope. 'No one's told me anything.'

'Well, Maggie, our news is that he's been spotted and is being tailed by the police, who are waiting for Andy to arrive.'

'I can't believe it! Let me try to find out. I'll ring and get in touch with Andy. Ring me back in ten minutes.'

Shaking, I replaced the receiver and took a deep breath. Alastair came into the room and told me that it was the police from Lochmaddy who had been on the phone earlier. They had asked if Andy was there and had then hung up.

My hands were sweating as I dialled the number for the police station in Lochmaddy. It was answered by Sergeant Anderson's wife, who exclaimed, 'It's true, Maggie. They're all out after him now, after he was spotted this morning. A crofter phoned in to say that he had heard a strange crying sound outside his window and when he looked outside it was Hercules. But the cattle in the field had heard him, too, and, when they came to have a look, he took fright and they chased him away, poor beastie.' She went on: 'Andy didn't want to build your hopes up again until he was quite sure for himself, so he's out there at the moment.'

'My God!' I thought out loud. 'Can I believe it?' I was quivering like a jelly, as I told Alastair the news. I wanted to scream with joy. I grew hot and cold and the phone started ringing again. It seemed that the media had all heard the news and they sounded just as excited as I was. In their own way they had all been involved in our disaster and seemed to have a special place in their hearts for Hercules. They all offered me a seat on their various planes, and, needless to say, I accepted the first offer.

I stumbled about in my haste to get dressed. As I flung some old clothes into a bag my mind screamed, 'Calm down, calm down, it's probably a false alarm.' I grabbed Alastair, who hobbled to the car as fast as he could on a broken leg, and we sped towards Glasgow. I think a broken leg was the least of poor Alastair's problems as he turned paler by the mile, grimly hanging on, with eyes staring ahead, as I tore through the outskirts of Glasgow in my desperate bid to catch the plane.

As we arrived at the airport, I jumped out of the car and Alastair took over the controls, thankful it was an automatic, with a relieved sigh. 'Good luck, Maggie,' he said as he drove off sedately. The weather was getting steadily worse and the cloud level was very low, but the pilot decided that he could make it and soon we were airborne.

As we approached the runway on Benbecula and taxied

towards the control tower, we could see that the tiny airfield was already crowded with small planes, such as our own, which had brought scores of reporters and photographers to the scene of the final chase. It all looked like a scene from a Humphrey Bogart film, as the terminal filled with the familiar faces of the journalists. All were eager for a good story or the best picture. Yet all these supposedly hard-nosed, seen-it-all-before reporters wanted a happy ending to their story. All the taxis the island could supply were mustered and, incredibly, the chase was on again. Archie, our special taxi driver, greeted me with tears in his eyes, genuine delight at the reappearance of Hercules shining through his ruddy face, as we set off to find Andy.

We went round the island, up one road and down the other, reporters crammed six to a car or more, only to find the ever-cheerful Sergeant Anderson and his men soaked to the skin, scrambling down a hill through the heather.

'We spotted him all right, Maggie,' he said, 'but some idiot frightened him off with their car. He's taken to the hills, up in all that mist.' He made a sweeping movement towards the skyline with his arm. 'We've lost Andy, too, but he's hardy, he'll be OK,' he finished reassuringly. The press all pounced on the Sergeant and his men, who, though exhausted, posed good-naturedly for the photographers.

It was five o'clock before we finally caught up with Andy at the whitewashed post office and store at Clachan, and, after I had almost crushed him to death with my hugs and kisses, he confirmed what Sergeant Anderson had already told us, but added ruefully, 'But he's scared. Completely on the defensive. I think we're going to have to tranquillise him, or he's going to get hurt.'

Darkness was closing in earlier than usual because of all the mist and rain, and there was nothing much more that we could do other than to organise ourselves for the next morning. But all the time at the back of our minds was the thought that it had seemed just as straightforward on the day that he had disappeared. Even then, with the soldiers, dogs, the helicopter and planes, we had not been able to find him. We prayed that night that fate would be kinder to us this time.

God moves in a mysterious way, and I will always believe that he had a hand in bringing Hercules back to us. At my aunt's house that night as we sat round the peat fire, we received a telephone call from a complete stranger called Allan Mann. He happened to be the owner of a company called Allan Mann Helicopters Ltd, and he was up in the north of Scotland when he had heard of the day's events on the radio. He thought that he might be the solution to our problems and, like an answer to our prayer, he offered us the use of one of his helicopters together with the services of one of his pilots, Captain Akroyd–Hunt, who'd had nine years' experience in Africa tracing and capturing game. It seemed too good to be true.

Next morning the helicopter made its noisy arrival at exactly 11 a.m. On board was our old friend Eddie Orbell and George Rafferty, the vet from the wildlife park. It all seemed miraculous, just like the script of an implausible Hollywood film. Allan and his pilot quickly refuelled the helicopter and were soon airborne again, with Eddie and George still on board. Soon the helicopter was joined by a fleet of small press planes as they set off in pursuit of Hercules.

Everyone's hopes were high, as they scoured the ground for the first sight of Hercules. But as the day wore on there was still no sign of him. It was hard to believe, but it seemed as though it was all going wrong again.

Andy waited at the pier at Lochmaddy with my father and the coach. My dad had rather hurriedly dashed up from the Inn and had crossed over on the ferry to North Uist with Mum in the passenger seat, the operator, Caledonian MacBrayne, kindly delaying the ferry so that they could get across. My mother waited at her old home with my bemused grandfather, who couldn't understand what all the fuss was about.

It would soon be time to call a halt to the day's search, and the helicopter would have to fly back to the mainland, and we would be left to face the awful task of searching for Hercules on our own again.

I was flying with Bob Ford-Sagers again, and, like the others, we had not seen a single trace of Hercules all day. As we taxied into the airfield to refuel, we saw that most of the other planes were there for the same reason and some had simply given up. We had been in the air for more than four hours and my eyes were strained from endless searching. I could see only a blur as we made our way to the control tower to join the other despondent crews who were talking in groups, swapping theories, about the puzzling day's search.

Suddenly the controller called for silence, and, as we

eagerly turned towards him, we could see him holding one hand up in the air as he pressed the earphones closer to his head. Then we heard the news we had all been waiting for – a crackling transmission from the helicopter crew saying, 'We've spotted him.'

I felt as though my heart would burst. It was beating so hard as more details began to filter through. 'He's running scared,' said the pilot. 'But we've got to get him now. We're going to use the tranquilliser gun or we'll lose him.' A tremendous cheer went up in the crowded smoke-filled room and everyone started to scramble outside. Press people fell over each other as they rushed to planes and cars, and there were frantic shouts for telephones. Bob and I decided that we should try to get to the scene, just in case I could be of any help.

We got into the car and headed recklessly towards the north of the island, all the constraints of the past few hours suddenly unleashed.

To our dismay we discovered that the helicopter was hovering over boggy moorland and there were no through roads. It was yet another frustrating twist, so, unable to do anything to help, we headed back to the coach at Lochmaddy.

As we drove back I watched anxiously as the bright-orange helicopter lifted and appeared on the skyline with a dark shape hanging below it. My imagination conjured up a thousand things that might still go wrong. 'What if the rope snaps or the net breaks?' I thought as the helicopter swept across the sky, pursued by the ravening hordes of journalists, camera lenses glittering as they captured the dramatic event on film.

The helicopter was hovering over the playground in Lochmaddy, just as Bob and I came into the town. From a distance I saw Andy's arms outstretched towards the pathetic bundle. He loosened the net, and Hercules was gently lowered into the back of the pickup truck. My father was at the wheel and he speedily drove Andy and the unconscious Hercules to the coach, where he was quickly transferred to the safety of his den.

It seemed as if every inhabitant of the island was there, and they surged around the coach to catch a glimpse of the bear that had captured their hearts over the past few weeks. I struggled through the crowds and was at last reunited with the son that I had given up for lost. Andy was bent over him, kissing his big black nose, crying unashamedly. He was not alone, for everyone present seemed to be crying, and only George Rafferty appeared to be calm amid the chaos as he administered the antidote to the powerful tranquilliser that had been used to subdue the terrified Hercules.

A few minutes after the shot had been put into his much-diminished rump, Hercules opened a bleary eye and gave his dad a great big sloppy kiss. With that he dropped off into a deep sleep.

With tear-stained faces Andy and I tried to thank the men responsible for Hercules's safe return, and found ourselves hopelessly inadequate in expressing our gratitude. Eddie explained that one of the helicopter crew had spotted Herc's ear jutting out from behind a large rock and, as they approached to take a closer look, sheer terror had made him bolt. After running at great speed he had dived into the middle of a peaty loch, and had stayed in the middle completely out of sight, apart from his head bobbing on the surface. The helicopter then had to swoop down low over the surface of the water, whipping up waves as they tried to herd him onto the surrounding moorland.

Once driven out of the small loch, Hercules started to run again and Eddie fired a shot with the tranquilliser gun, but missed because the draught from the rotor blades blew it off course. His second shot, however, went straight into Hercules's rump. Under the unabating pressure Hercules decided to try to hide again and so made promptly for a deep crevice. There he lay quite still, huddled among the heather.

The helicopter landed and kept its engines running. Eddie and George leapt out, uncertain whether Hercules was by now unconscious or still conscious and sufficiently terrified to turn on them. They managed to put a rope around his neck, but as they did so and Hercules felt the rope tighten, he was up and running again, driven on by fear alone. He dragged his two captors behind him as he charged up the face of a steep hill, but as the drug at last began to take effect, he ground to a halt and collapsed. He was quickly rolled into the strong net, which was attached to a cable from the helicopter, and unceremoniously lifted into the air and back to Lochmaddy and safety.

We thanked the helicopter crew from the bottom of our hearts, for without them it was doubtful whether Hercules would have survived. The drama was now over and the crew returned to the mainland, the heroes of the day.

Hercules had been missing for twenty-four days and the effects on him were massive. He had suffered a dramatic, almost fatal loss of weight, having lost at least 20 stone since he had disappeared. He now looked like an empty and rather moth-eaten fur coat as he lay huddled at the back of the coach, and we placed a large pillow beneath his head to make him as comfortable as possible.

It was obvious that Hercules had eaten nothing. Far from ravaging the countryside, the poor frightened softy had not even killed so much as a rabbit in order to satisfy what must have been an agonising hunger.

That evening his sleep was so deep that he did not even flinch as I administered the second shot of antidote, and we began to worry that he might be so far gone with exhaustion and hunger that he could not pull through. He should by now have been well awake and neither of us slept as we wondered whether his health would stand the strain.

Next morning Hercules still had not woken, and we could see the bloodsucking ticks that covered his mangy fur. We attacked them with tweezers and disinfectant and, as we removed them, they left Herc's skin covered in ugly sores. Meanwhile, Hercules was oblivious to the world.

A constant stream of well-wishers came to the coach bringing with them parcels of Hercules's favourite foods – beans, yogurt, grapes – and, when he eventually woke up later that morning, we tried to tempt him with them.

Poor Hercules could not eat a thing. Even the eggs and prawns that he loved so much failed to interest him. He seemed to be unable to chew and anything put into his mouth would pathetically spill out again.

We finally left him to sleep some more, and, worrying what we could do next, we left the coach and walked to my grandfather's house, some 20 yards away. He was still bemused by all the bustling activity that was going on around him and sat puffing his pipe, waiting patiently for Aunt Effie to produce tea and scones for him.

'Haf you tried him with milk yet, Margaret?' Aunt Effie asked me in her strong Highland accent.

'He doesn't like milk much, Effie,' Andy replied, shaking his head, while the rest of the household looked on with interest at this new suggestion. 'He'll only ever take milk in his tea and coffee.'

'Oh, now, I think you should be trying him with some just in case,' persisted Effie in her best schoolteacher's voice, as she turned to say to her husband's brother, 'Archie-John, away and get the cow milked to see if poor Hercules will take some fresh warm milk.'

Archie-John dutifully rose from the table, painfully shy in front of such a crowd, and carried the white enamel bucket with him to the byre opposite the house, shouting for the cow as he went. The cow ambled slowly after him and minutes later Archie-John, head bowed, reappeared carrying the bucket now full of steaming fresh milk.

We all got up and made our way in single file out of the back door and walked to the coach. The smell of peat lingered in our nostrils as we tried Hercules with the still-warm milk. Success! Like a small calf, he slowly started to suck at the milk in the bottom of the bucket and, as he seemed to know that it was doing him some good, he greedily slurped at it until every drop was gone. Once again, his inbuilt common sense was helping him to survive.

At last we could begin to relax completely in the knowledge that, when Hercules was well, *all* was well. He was still very weak, but his thirst for milk could not be contained or supplied and so the call went out: 'The Big Softy needs milk.' Supplies started to arrive from all sources, in jugs, buckets, basins and bottles. He drank 40 pints in two days, and all but drank the island dry.

By now, he was able to sit up and watch as visitors came from all over the islands, old and young, and he even managed to entice from her cottage an old woman who had not left her home in almost twenty years.

Amid all the well-wishers was a very sorry-looking Sergeant Anderson, who whispered to Andy, 'Could I have a wee word in private with you?' Andy, of course, agreed and we both made our way to the house, where Sergeant Anderson told us of his dilemma. 'I've had orders from headquarters in Inverness – this isn't from me, mind,' he said, 'but you've to get off the island on the first available boat, and we've to charge you for being here with Hercules.' He heaved a sigh and continued: 'It's a piece of nonsense, a bloody disgrace if you ask me, but I'm sorry, Andy, orders are orders.'

'Well, Sergeant,' said Andy, 'you go ahead and charge us, but there's no way we're going until we've been round the schools to let the kids see Hercules.'

'But Andy,' said the exasperated sergeant, 'I've to charge you for every day you stay on the islands.' He then proceeded to pull out his little black book and told us our rights. Poor Sergeant Anderson! He had worked so hard to get Hercules safely back to us, and now he was having to carry out some orders from an uninvolved police department on the mainland. We almost thought he would turn mutinous. The Sergeant completed his business and left, still a good friend despite the charges.

No sooner had the word got out than the loyal islanders began to rally round to give us their full support. Naturally, the press picked up the news and began to run articles about the absurdity of the charges, and Caledonian MacBrayne, the ferry company, made Hercules an honorary member, saying that he could travel on their ferries whenever he liked and for free. The ferry employees even said that, if Hercules was not allowed to stay on the island for as long he wanted, nobody would be allowed on or off!

Soon the campaign began to snowball and Andy obtained the services of Joe Beltrami, Scotland's answer to the USA's famous TV lawyer Perry Mason, to defend Hercules. Joe immediately took up the question of the charges against us with the Procurator Fiscal (in Scotland, the legal officer who acts as public prosecutor and coroner). We were charged with having a dangerous animal on the island and allowing it to escape.

As far as the first charge was concerned, we had a Performing Animals Licence, which meant that we did not need a licence for a dangerous animal; and we thought the second charge was equally unfair, as we had not *intended* to lose Hercules and it was obvious we had done everything in our power to find him.

The Procurator Fiscal was clearly not happy with the charges, and, so Joe said, he would be prepared to let us off if we applied for a Dangerous Animals Licence. Andy wanted to contest the charges in court but was eventually persuaded by Joe Beltrami that it would not be a good idea to have any blemish on Hercules's record, and as we had more bother with the authorities in London a little later on we agreed to obtain an additional (and unnecessary) licence and the charges were dropped.

Before we left the island we made a tour of the schools, driving slowly so that Hercules had a smooth ride. Some of the schools had fewer than ten pupils, and, when they saw Hercules, the smiles that covered their faces seemed to make all our ordeals worthwhile.

It was with great sadness that we left the islands, having found there nothing but a fondness and generosity that we will always remember.

But we wanted to get home to complete Hercules's recovery.

CHAPTER 9

OUR CHANGING LIVES

It took several months for Hercules to regain his lost weight and recover physically from his ordeal – mentally, his hurts were expressed in a touching reluctance to leave our company.

I fed him as one would an invalid during the weeks following our return home. Foods that were easily digested: steamed fish and mince, milk, yogurt and plenty of eggs. He spent a lot of time in our sitting room, resting in front of the fire and watching television, and he liked to have Andy or me with him as much as possible. His spirits were high, though, and it didn't look as if any permanent damage of a serious kind had been done.

He was frightened of open spaces. It was all right so long as we were about to give him confidence and make him feel secure, but now he would not even go into the paddock on his own. He was clearly scared that what happened to him might happen again.

Another change in him that would have been amusing if it hadn't been so tragic, and such a vivid reminder of what he must have gone through, was his absolute refusal to jump into deep water. Before, he liked nothing better than to dive into a swimming pool or a loch. Now, he furtively found the shallow end of the pool and tested the water for depth with his paw. Unless he could feel or see the bottom he would not go in.

That summer, Andy and Herc were playing around a swimming pool, chasing each other and romping. Andy would dive in, and poor Hercules so much wanted to join him. He teetered on the edge, time after time, but then always ran down to the steps at the shallow end before entering the pool. We hadn't tried him in salt water since his time in the wild, and were afraid that he might not take too happily to it, but swimming was still his favourite sport.

He preferred to have people about him – as many people as possible – and enjoyed himself best indoors. He especially enjoyed being in crowded places such as theatres, where he gained security from the numbers.

This was a good thing. After his return from the edge of the world Hercules was a very famous bear indeed. There could have been few people in the whole country who had not heard of him. We were swamped with letters of support and interest, presents and cards, and thousands of visitors. Among the mail came numerous invitations to perform, both in studios and in public theatres, including invitations for several TV shows. Had Hercules not been happy about being indoors we would have been unable to introduce him to his admiring public.

One of the major assignments we were offered that winter was to take part in a big variety show in the Playhouse Theatre in Edinburgh with Lena Zavaroni. It would be the most sustained test of Herc's talents so far, as we were billed to perform twice a day for three weeks.

Everybody concerned was very aware that Hercules might not be interested. Quite apart from his ordeal being only three months before, we had to take him up six flights of stairs to reach the stage. Our contract had been carefully worded to take account of the fact that Herc could not be coerced into doing anything he did not want to do. If he didn't like a project then he was intelligent enough to work out a way of putting a spanner in the works, as he had done when we muzzled him against his will and expected him to wrestle.

We were hopeful, however. If we hadn't been, we would never have taken on the job. Hercules's faith in us was so complete by now that we felt sure he would trust us, and once he became used to the unfamiliar situation we were sure that he would enjoy it. Nevertheless, to expect an animal to come up trumps so often, for so long, might be to expect the impossible. If it came off it would be a sensational achievement.

And come off it did, well beyond our expectations. Understandably, Hercules was a bit nervous to begin with:

never before had there been so many people around him and, although we knew he was fond of music – especially loud music, which he would listen to from his den as it wafted out of the kitchen – never before had he worked with an orchestra.

From the start, however, everything went perfectly. He romped up the worrying six flights of stairs. He quickly stole the hearts of all the people involved in the production. And, after being initially intrigued by the orchestra and the music, he soon devoted his attention to the audience. Needless to say, the audience loved him.

The orchestra were on the stage behind Andy and Hercules, separated from them by a gauze curtain so that the sound they made was not hindered, and yet they could be invisible if the scene required it.

The musicians became quite used to sharing the stage with an almost full-grown grizzly bear and had the security of the gauze curtain between him and them, for what it was worth. Hercules became a great favourite with them. Then, on the last day of the show's run, he gave an incredible demonstration of his feelings towards them, which was also an uncanny indication of how aware he was of all that went on around him, and of how talented he was at upstaging everybody else.

By the third week, everyone was well into the routine of the production, and, although Hercules varied his performance daily and was never predictable, he had grown completely accustomed to what was expected of him.

Perhaps it was the sense of excitement that always

accompanies the end of a successful show for those taking part in it, perhaps it was pure bravado on Hercules's part, but, whatever it was, suddenly, towards the end of the act, he reared up on his hind legs, raised his arms above his head and made a beeline for the gauze curtain separating him from the orchestra. Over 8 feet of grizzly bear is enough to fill even the stoutest heart with terror, even when the stout hearts concerned have been working alongside the bear for the previous three weeks. The music ended with many odd squeaks and groans. The orchestra panicked and many tried to escape. Music stands were overturned and chaos ensued. And then the cause of all the fuss calmly stepped back again and swaggered over to his partner.

When it became apparent that the whole thing was 'part of the act' the audience were convulsed, and, once they had recovered their composure, so too were the members of the orchestra.

It was clear that Hercules knew exactly what he was doing. He had had the last laugh again, and quite literally brought the house down.

Along with the greetings and invitations came honours and awards. The *Daily Mirror* made him Fatty of the Month and its Personality of the Year. He became Scottish TV Personality of the Year, as well, and the Scottish Tourist Board gave him a special award, 'To the Bear with Flair', for bringing so much publicity to the Western Isles. Heineken gave him their Christmas award as the most 'Refreshing Personality of the Year', and he was made an honorary member of countless clubs and societies, including one called the Teddy Bears of the World Club. He won a 'humanitarian award' from Animals in America for 'failing to harm any wildlife whilst starving'. The Cartoonists' Club of Great Britain gave him their supreme accolade, the Gold Joker of the Year, for the number of humorous drawings that he had inspired, such as the one in which he was shown sharing a pint with the locals at the pub in Creagorry.

At the time he collected this particular award, in the Cartoonists' Club off Fleet Street, we were being hounded by an officious man from the council who believed he had a personal mission to prevent Hercules being seen in public in London. He had been following us around all day, trying to frighten people that we were visiting by telling them that they would be charged if they allowed Hercules into their premises or onto their shows. He arrived at the Cartoonists' Club with a band of policemen, and, leaving them outside, dashed in to use the telephone. For what reason we didn't stop to find out, for as soon as he was spotted he was surrounded by a mob of our friends in the press, who succeeded in keeping him trapped in the callbox until the award had been presented and received. He emerged furious and, shortly afterwards, we were cautioned by the police and later summoned to Bow Street Magistrates' Court for not having a Dangerous Animals Licence. It was obvious that it was time to take get some serious help!

We contacted Hercules's lawyer, Joe Beltrami, and he took the advice of senior counsel, who said it was quite clear that we didn't need a licence as we already had a

Performing Animals Licence. However, Mr Beltrami advised us that, since there was no law against having both licences, we should go ahead and get one, which would not only satisfy the English court but would persuade the Procurator Fiscal in Inverness to drop his case. We agreed to his suggestions and went ahead and applied for the much talked-about document.

So now Hercules had all the possible licences a bear could need, and he still had no criminal record.

For the next couple of years we travelled all across Great Britain making public appearances at shows and on TV, appearing in a Bond move, *Octopussy*, with Roger Moore, and starring in a Christmas panto at the Playhouse Theatre in Edinburgh. It was really enjoyable meeting Hercules's adoring fans, who turned up in their droves to see our Big Fellow. We have many memories of these times but one of the loveliest was an occasion that happened after that theatre debut at the Playhouse. One morning a lady phoned the Sheriffmuir Inn to speak to us. She enquired if she could possibly bring her daughter, who was blind, to meet Herc. They had both been to the Christmas show at the Playhouse and her daughter had heard our show on stage and was desperate to touch Hercules and be close to him. 'Of course she can,' we informed her. What was to follow was one of the most magical things I'd ever seen.

It was a cold, misty February morning that mother and daughter turned up at the Inn to meet Herc. The young lady in question was in her late teens, with long dark hair. After a chat we could see she really wasn't interested in anything else but meeting our Big Fellow. So, while we waited in the kitchen, Andy went out and brought Hercules in. All the time the young lady chattered away excitedly. Hercules's big bulky frame suddenly filled the doorway of the kitchen and he took a quick look around as if to say, 'OK, what's going on?' Andy brought him into the middle of the room and asked him to sit beside the girl, which he quickly did. I held her hand, which was shaking with excitement, and said, 'Right, that's Herc beside you now. He's a big guy, so just be careful and you'll be fine.' Of course being blind gave her a heightened awareness of touch and she eagerly moved towards her new furry friend to stand behind him.

Hercules was always inquisitive and liked to be getting on with things but that morning he was very gentle and quiet. He seemed to sense that she was special and needed some time as he sat and she gently stroked him. Her hands caressed his big furry body around his ears, round his neck, down his back. She ran her hands along his arms and held his paw. 'Just be careful,' I said as she was becoming almost too confident but as I spoke she leaned forward between his ears with her chin, his big back pressing against her body, and she ran her hands all over his face, right down over his big wet nose to his mouth – and I must say, at that point, my heart was in mine.

It was quite a weird, surreal situation, as normally Hercules would have wanted to play, but on this occasion he just sat rock still as if aiding her in her quest. Not one movement did he make. I was so filled with awe at his inherent ability to work out a situation like that. Yet another magical moment

Left: Partial to a shandy.

Below: It's a grand life!

(*Glasgow Herald*)

Left: Think you're a big guy?

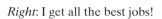

Right: I get all the best jobs!

Left: Andy and Herc on the set of the movie *Pathfinder*.

Left: Mmm, that looks good.

Right: Off out with Mum

Left: Swimtime.

Left: Take my picture.

Right: A bowler hat for
my visit to Sandringham.
(*Lynn News and Advertiser*)

Herc found the paint pot!

Right: Little Henry keeps his distance.
(*Sunday People*)

Left: Time for a ride out.
(*Leslie Lane, AIIP*)

Right: Let's have some fun, Dad!

Above: Gotcha!

Below left: Pool time with the boys.

Below right: Just the two of us.

Christmas with the Robins.

he had created in our lives. Eventually, after the obligatory cup of tea, mum and daughter left the Inn, delighted with their own precious memory.

CHAPTER 10

LET'S ALL GO STATESIDE!

During the following months Andy's endless sense of adventure sprang to the fore once more. 'I think we should go to America for a while and see what they think of big Herc in the land of the bears.' Rather an awesome prospect, I thought.

Over the next few weeks we sat and discussed the pros and cons of a trip to the States. Eventually, I found myself swept up in the thought of a new adventure and started to enquire into the possibility of all three of us travelling to the States. Andy had wrestled there many years before and knew his way around, so it wasn't an alien prospect to him.

Off he went to Los Angeles and New York while Herc and I stayed at home eagerly awaiting an update on the possibilities. Yes, we could travel if we secured the appropriate visas and licences. How we would get there was quite a different matter. Diligently, I did my homework and found out whom I should be in contact with. The initial response was, as you can imagine, at first, surprise and disbelief, but when I explained that obviously all three of us would have to travel together in Hercules's coach, as we were not prepared to have him transported in a crate, it was hard to be taken seriously.

Originally, in the planning, the obvious choice was that we would take him (naturally) in a Hercules jet, which we felt would not only be appropriate but was the biggest transporter we knew of. It turned out, though, that even the giant jet was too small for Hercules's mobile home. But, once an idea takes root in your head, it's hard to get rid of it and it has just got to be allowed to grow. We decided, therefore, that we would travel with our big furry bundle and go the long way round by sea. Who would take us, though? That was the problem. Fortunately, it was not long until we found a container company, the Blue Star Line, which was willing to oblige us. Now it was all systems go.

The weather at Sheriffmuir was drawing in, heralding the cold winters that we normally faced on top of the hills. As usual, I had to attend to all the finer details, and so I set about preparing for our move. We sold the Inn, keeping a field to build on when we came back from our adventure. Over the following weeks I packed and labelled all our movable possessions in the coach, all stored under the giant floor compartments, and everything else went into storage. Hercules's wrestling ring was manoeuvred into the back of the grey Transit van Andy had bought for the purpose: it was to be shipped with us in a container.

As all the preparations at home were going on, there was much to do to meet our accommodation needs in America. Andy had managed to acquire a plot of land in a secluded spot just north of Los Angeles at New Hall: Sunshine Mountain. We went back and forward to arrange for Hercules's enclosure to be built. It was all to be built to code and consisted of a fantastic swimming pool and Jacuzzi, a nice sitting room for Herc all enclosed in a lovely pink block wall to keep him safe. All fit for a star. Andy and I would live in our coach on the property and we put the big fella first, as usual, in the comfort stakes.

The final days leading up to the adventure were nerve-racking and, as for me, I became rather sad. Trailing a grizzly bear across the world would be a very serious responsibility indeed. The reality is, you can't just up sticks and leave if you don't like it. It took a lot of careful planning to keep our big fella safe. On my side of things, the realisation dawned of the enormity of what we were about to do. Our family had always been very close. My mum and dad, grandma, brothers and sisters, all the people I loved, weren't going to be just down the road any more. My mind ran riot. 'What if something happens to any of them while I'm away on the other side of the world?' I thought. 'What if something happens to us, and they're not near at hand?'

I think for the first time in my life it dawned on me how much all of the things you can take for granted in life mattered – and I loved my family and friends dearly: my wee mum, a quiet islander from Uist, always feeding and caring for us all and asking nothing in return; my dad, her best friend, who, to be quite honest, had really never got over the shock of his eldest daughter bringing home the larger-than-life wrestler with his shirt opened across his vast tanned chest, not the farmer he had most probably hoped for; my younger brothers and sisters, all of whom I loved but sometimes forgot to show it to; and Grandma, with her old-fashioned tilt on life and her funny little anecdotes. What on earth were we doing?

But we were on course, our route was planned, and the three of us prepared to face new horizons.

CHAPTER 11
OUR JOURNEY BEGINS

In the days before we left Sheriffmuir on our epic journey, I felt nervous and sick in my stomach. Andy, though, was ploughing on enthusiastically. Things between us became tense, not ideal in the circumstances. The day came to leave, all the goodbyes were said, and we set off from the Inn to the docks at Felixstowe with Hercules taking it all in his stride – as usual. TV cameras followed us and recorded our departure. We were off!

People waved at the coach when they realised who was on board. I waved back but my heart was heavy, with more than a little doubt setting in as we motored away from home.

After a long journey, we reached Felixstowe docks later that evening and there was a clamber from the big burly dockers to see Herc, some of them returning in the dark of night with their children in tow.

One thing we were fortunate enough to learn through our dealings with ordinary people who were keen to meet our big fella Hercules was that everyone matters, absolutely everyone. Andy and I always took time to talk and to let people know how much their support and interest meant to us. Through this we learned that, on the whole, people are kind and caring and in the main have goodness in their hearts. This appreciation we gained of our fellow human beings has guided the rest of our lives. It's great to feel what a smile and a chat can achieve – and it doesn't cost a thing.

The next day dawned; the busy dock clunked and rattled as containers were moved into place and lifted high onto their designated ships.

Soon, it was our turn. Herc looked on, interested in all that was going on around him. We were escorted to the side of the giant container ship, and, as all the dockers mingled round pointing and chatting, Andy insisted that, if Hercules was being heaved into place aloft, he would be in the coach with him. But the officials were horrified. 'Not a chance!' they said. If the coach plunged to the ground during the operation it would be catastrophic for both Andy and Herc. But, no, Andy insisted and jumped into the coach with his boy. This set everyone scurrying about, paperwork in hand, shaking heads and waving arms in disbelief.

As usual, though, Andy had his way. The large crane used to lift the heavy loads was moved into place over the coach. My heart was in my mouth as I quietly took in everything that going on around us. I needn't have worried, as, effort-lessly, the 'Hercmobile', as we called it, was swung into the air, Andy waving in the back with our boy.

They were quickly on board and swiftly shackled to the top deck behind the officers' quarters (where we ate and relaxed during the trip). When I look back on it, I still remember the relief I felt. We were on board and in place in what was to be our home for the next three and a half weeks.

CHAPTER 12

CALIFORNIA, HERE WE COME!

Our journey with Hercules was not uneventful. Heavy seas in the English Channel made for a rough ride on the *California Star*. Huge as she was, she was just a speck against the natural forces of the sea, but, as we crossed the Atlantic and skirted the Azores, all three of us became calmer and were at last enjoying the passage.

As soon as Hercules had arrived on board, he'd become a firm favourite with the crew, who gathered round to meet the furry guy they'd come to call 'BH' or 'Big Herc'. Each morning when we rose we would find secret parcels that the chefs and galley crew had left hidden under the chassis of the coach. The hotter the days became, the more ice cream seemed to find its way up to the top deck, with Hercules relishing every lick. The Purser was going crazy and was on a mission to find out who the food thieves were, but his efforts were foiled at every turn by the crew, who were dodging and working things to Herc's advantage. They easily led the Purser a merry dance.

As the heat grew more intense we were worried how Hercules would cope, but nature and Herc's canny mind let him just take it easy, and he was neither up nor down with the heat.

The days passed and we had settled into a routine of play and relaxation, topped up periodically, of course, with every flavour of ice cream imaginable. Inevitably, the ship was running short of this delightful commodity and we often had to dive into the coach when we saw the Purser surging towards us with his clipboard of ship's rations, and tried to hide the telltale signs of indulgence that surrounded Hercules's mouth. I think the Purser's puzzled expression lasted throughout the entire trip – it still makes me laugh to think about it.

As our trip progressed the ship became the world you lived and breathed in, relaxed in and had a feeling of belonging to. It is easy to understand now how men 'escape' to a life at sea: it feels like no one, and nothing, but nature can touch you.

Not many bears have travelled through the Panama Canal, and on the night before we were due to traverse its steamy wonders we waited in the Panama Basin with the other ships ready to roll in the early morning. We arrived at the first lock. The heat was intense and the dock was buzzing with excitement. Hercules had admirers even in Panama and the canal pilots were quickly on board to meet him, holding copies of the Panamanian newspaper.

He made the front page as usual. It was strange when things like that happened: it made us realise the scope of Hercules's fame; it always woke us up from what was, for us, the normal day-to-day relationship we had with our Big Bear to the enormity and uniqueness of our lives. It's a strange thing, but when you are in the midst of a situation on a daily basis, it is simply your life – but it doesn't seem at all normal to the outside world. Once again, Hercules rose to the occasion and was delighted to meet and greet and pose for pictures with his newest fans. Smiling broadly and waving, they disembarked and we were on our way through the canal.

What a beautiful and wondrous sight that canal was. The heat hit you like a wall and the smells and sounds were so rich and raw that they enveloped your senses completely. After about twenty-four hours we were through and off on the final leg towards San Pedro docks, Los Angeles, passing Acapulco starboard side.

At last, Los Angeles was within striking distance, and the calm feeling that had taken hold on board was replaced by a nervous restlessness of what was to come.

The docks at San Pedro were packed with TV cameras and crews, all vying for an interview with the three Scots travellers who were about to disembark upon their shores. In this neck of the woods, the film capital of the world, our crazy dream sparked their interest like some sort of Disney movie, and somehow, as we peered down from the deck, it all made sense.

Through customs and immigration we went, all our documents thankfully in place. Under the watchful eyes of the officials, who showed us great kindness mixed with bewilderment, our first steps on American soil were at least reassuring. The final part of our journey to Hercules's quarters at Sunshine Mountain was beginning.

CHAPTER 13

OUR YEAR IN THE CITY OF ANGELS

The year passed quickly and we all enjoyed the use of Hercules's pool and Jacuzzi in the baking heat of the Californian summer. We worked with our agent on Sunset Boulevard and our lawyers guided us through the dos and don'ts of US procedures. We were now in the land of the bears. The Americans had a very different slant on us from that of Hercules's adoring public back home. In America, of course, deaths and injuries from bear attacks were common. They don't treat bears as pets, and certainly not as a family member. They were more used to hearing horror stories of campers being mauled and eaten and, because of that, they had a great respect for the mighty bear.

We were very lucky and kept busy, and Hercules flitted

from one TV studio to another with great ease, wearing only his little collar and his tartan necktie.

Probably our proudest moment during our American stay came one balmy evening when Hercules made an appearance at The Greek Theatre in Los Angeles. It is a great outdoor amphitheatre that can seat 7,000 people in the audience. We had been contacted by the powers-that-be of the University of California, Los Angeles – better known as UCLA – a famous and giant campus. Its mascot for the college was a bear, but in all its years of existence the college had never been in a position to present a real live bear: it was to be a surprise appearance.

After many meetings and a journey to the Pauley Pavilion, an Olympic venue on the campus, terms and conditions for Hercules's safety were agreed. He was to be their first live mascot. Initially, the Los Angeles Fire Department told us that we would have to chain Hercules to the stage. 'No way!' said Andy indignantly. 'That's not going to happen. He'll wear his wee tartan tie and that's it, or we can't do it.'

At first, we thought that *would* be it, and that it would be a no-go. No way did we think the Fire Department would sway from its original decision. However, some major strings were pulled, it seems, and the Department was willing to allow Herc to be free on stage with 500 students – quite a risk on their part.

'We will all be there watching,' said the department chief.

We ourselves were confident that Hercules would not 'eat anybody', but it was a pretty brave decision that the Department took.

On the morning of the event we drove to the theatre and had a quiet look at the giant stage. The event was called Spring Sing, when, at the end of term, the students (the Bruins) put on a show. After checking everything out, we sneaked off to hide away until the evening event started. Only the university establishment and the local fire authorities knew that we would be making an appearance that night.

The day passed, sunny and warm, with the three of us hiding away from sight, tucked under some cooling trees with the air conditioning running at full blast. Hercules had had his morning swim and was quite happy to relax with us and share a coffee. But it was soon time to get the show on the road. We started up the coach and slowly made our way back to the theatre, where we were quietly installed at the loading docks behind the stage.

The show was well under way as we drew up and the noise was almost overwhelming as we met the enthusiastic but nervous representatives from the university. Bands played, strobe lights lit the balmy night sky and the audience whistled and cheered as the entertainment went on.

Andy and I had had a run-through during our earlier visit that day, but I had a good few butterflies fluttering about in my tummy as we prepared for our entrance stage left. Hercules, of course, was as usual up for it. 'No problem,' he seemed to say. 'Where are we off to now?' So, without further ado, when they called us forward he clambered up the loading bay keen to see what all the noise was about.

From his upbringing at Sheriffmuir and his subsequent escapades, Herc was well used to being surrounded by people, and that night there sure were plenty of them. Knowing him well, Andy and I didn't doubt for a minute that he would just stroll onto the stage comfortable in the knowledge that, 'If Mum and Dad are with me, I'll be OK.' Suddenly, though, Andy felt him pull backwards on his rope as the huge stage filled with students and entertainers came into view. 'Oh, no!' he said urgently. 'He's pulling back, he must be frightened of all the noise.'

But, as we turned back to look at him, we realised fear had nothing to do with it. Hercules had spied all the leftover plastic cups with their contents of cola and the like. He was now simply helping himself to those contents, leaving one now and again if it was not to his taste. No panic. What a bear he was!

Heather Locklear, a glamorous blonde American actress, was presenting the show that evening. She asked for quiet, as she had a very important announcement to make. The audience were intrigued as she read out a telegram from President Ronald Reagan, a former student at UCLA. He was congratulating the University for at last managing to find itself a real live mascot.

A puzzled cheer erupted, growing in volume like a wave among the throngs that were gathered. What could be happening? Heads bobbed and turned. People gave each other puzzled glances. Then Heather proudly said, in her loudest voice, 'I'd like to introduce you to UCLA's new mascot, the magnificent Hercules the Bear.'

She turned to us, her arms outstretched, beckoning us from the wings. The whole place erupted. The brass band began to play. The strobe lights streaked the sky. And each and every one of the audience was applauding and stamping their feet. What an atmosphere that was – high-voltage.

To our delight our big, beautiful, furry man just ambled on stage with us, swaying his big bottom nonchalantly, and I must say, even amid that turmoil, he was probably the most relaxed I'd ever seen him. 'All these people – must be a party,' he seemed to be thinking as he rolled on his back and played with the microphone cable on the giant stage. He hugged both Andy and me with his big paws in front of that huge crowd. I was so proud of him that night.

We were congratulated by the people from the Fire Department. They said how nervous they had felt putting their necks on the line that evening, but they felt very relieved that they had made the right decision to let Hercules be himself and show his eager public what a fabulous big bear he was.

The UCLA authorities were over the moon. At last they had their mascot – and they had big plans for him. There was one problem, though, and, unfortunately, I was it. Much though I had enjoyed our trip and I felt delighted that we had proved to ourselves and to America that Herc was unique, I was not ready to put down roots in California. I missed my own country and was homesick for my family and friends, which, as life will teach us are irreplaceable. I learned through that trip that the familiar things in life *are* life, so I was ready make plans for the return trip home.

We had more offers: a film called *The Hotel New Hampshire,* TV work and of course the invitation for Herc to be the UCLA mascot. But it was time to leave. We had spent over a year in the USA, and Andy, too, had felt the need to return home. So it was back on the *California Star* for our return trip.

She sat waiting for us in the docks at San Pedro ready to cross the seas on the return journey. The crew were much the same and greeted us like long-lost friends, and happily stroked Herc once he was back on board. Predictable, as it may seem on that trip too, there proved to be a puzzling shortage of ice cream on board. Plans had been made for us to serve out the six months' quarantine period on our return at Edinburgh Zoo with the assistance of the lovely director, who helped us so much, Roger Wheater. He had special quarters built for Hercules beside the other two bears, which we of course paid for, and, as we drove into our beloved Edinburgh that first night home and turned into Corstorphine Road, it felt good, and a sense of quite contented relief took hold.

The giant metal zoo gates were opened for us and Andy ably manoeuvred his way up the fairly steep gradients of the zoo to Herc's new quarters. We were not allowed to disembark from the coach until the two Customs and Excise men had inspected it. They were waiting for us, documents in hand, and to say that they were rather overwhelmed at the task of frisking their first grizzly bear is an understatement, but it was a wonderful humorous touch on our first night home.

Hercules's enclosure consisted of a large building with a secondary skin of birdproof wire on the primary entrance.

The conditions that the zoo imposed on us meant we were able to play with him only before the zoo opened to the public (who flocked to see him) and after the zoo closed, as the officials did not want to encourage any members of the public to think that they might be able to 'pet' the other two bears in the next enclosure. So, after moving the coach into the car park behind the Post House Hotel beside the zoo, we all settled quickly into a daily routine.

At eight o'clock each and every morning for six months Andy and I would make our way from the coach to Hercules's temporary home with the breakfast and his coffee. We had to strictly observe the quarantine regulations and dip our feet in the disinfectant at his door before and after visiting him inside. Each day he greeted us with great relish. 'Ahh, Mum and Dad are back,' you could almost see him think. So we'd feed him, clean him and make sure that he had a good hour's rough and tough play with Andy and some big cuddles from me before the zoo opened for the day and an endless stream of admirers flocked to see him.

Throughout that six months we spent lots of time chatting to his fans as they peered in to get a closer look at the bear who had stolen their hearts. Hercules, as you will gather, liked his routine of breakfast, two snacks during the day and a dinner that was served after the zoo closed for the evening, at which time he also liked to have another good bit of soft play and some hugs. The two bears next door, especially the female, Mary, seemed to become very envious of all Herc's tasty meals and sniffed the air when they smelled food arriving.

Late in the evening, as night drew in every day for six months, there was a ritual: fish and chips from one of the chip shops on Corstorphine Road, where we would buy them and deliver them to Herc's quarters at about 10 p.m. with a bottle of his customary Irn-Bru to wash them down. Herc loved those fish and chips!

Every night, though, Mary would be waiting for us way down at the bottom of the wall of her enclosure with a very sad, begging face. Although it wasn't really our place we felt that we couldn't have that, so we would always bring her chips as well. Oh, what a treat that was for her! She never missed a night. Eventually, the newspapers announced that she and Herc were now an item.

The six months of quarantine rolled on from October till the end of March. Herc continued to be quite content with life and with meeting and greeting his many visitors. Andy and I stayed in the coach in the car park for the entire six months and, I must say, it was a thoroughly enjoyable and relaxing time with walks into and around the zoo and into Edinburgh, where we would have our customary bowl of soup or tea and a scone.

The zoo staff were always helpful and, though they doubted that we would stick to our task for every day of the six months, Roger Wheater admitted we did just that, marvelling at our commitment. He said he was proud to have been able to help with the facilities and had enjoyed having Hercules there.

The end of March arrived, and it was time to leave our temporary home. The mesh gates were opened for the first time in six months for Hercules, who ambled out with his big furry bottom wiggling as he walked up the stairs into his coach. As usual, the press and TV cameras were there to record it all and then we were off again.

Freedom for the three of us – happy to be together again as a family.

CHAPTER 14

BACK HOME

We had both decided that, after all the time that had passed, it would be a retrograde step to go back to Sheriffmuir, and so we accepted a kind offer from our good friend of many years, Sir Hugh Fraser, to stay at his estate in Killin. We remained there for nine months and travelled to all our jobs with Herc from the south of England to the very north of Scotland. Herc gained more and more fans, who arrived at the events to witness him and Andy wrestling while I played the part of referee – and in all that time and all those years Andy never won a single bout. Herc had him outwitted and outweighed at every turn. Of course, a bit of cheating would occasionally go on but I tried to turn a blind eye in the main, apart from when Herc would grab Andy's willy through his wrestling trunks, and I felt I had to announce in my sternest referee's voice, 'Public warning to Hercules for biting his daddy's willy!' It always brought the house down.

Between travelling to these shows we did lots of promotional work and TV and film appearances. One film in particular was shot near our home. We had since settled in a dower house at Auchenbowie near Stirling. The film was called *Pathfinder* and was produced by the Norwegian Government and an independent film company. The fixer, Per, a tall Norwegian, came to check things out and to see if this bear they had heard of was indeed as special as people said he was. Hercules didn't disappoint, and Per was thrilled that he was the perfect bear for the part, which was to be in a fairly violent historical story.

After scouting for a location he found one close at hand and asked Andy if he could play four different parts in the film and do the stunts, as he would have to wrestle and fight the 'wild bear'. Obviously, volunteers for that role were thin on the ground!

Everything was agreed and eventually a whole crew arrived for the week. For the location, some 'snow' was needed. They covered a nearby quarry in sheets that had been sewn together, and then placed some trees and boulders that they had brought with them from Norway on top of the sheets. The ground was covered with white gravel, which ran into the white of the sheets. It looked amazing! You could not tell that it wasn't real snow on a mountain.

Each day they arrived at the quarry and we would drive Hercules up to the site to meet them. Wardrobe and make-up people would clad Andy in various reindeer skins, as each part had a different colour of skin to make the whole thing look authentic. Herc was thoroughly enjoying himself in the limelight and would contentedly wait in the back of his coach until it was his turn to be included in a scene.

Every day for seven days, as the crew worked, he'd be in and out, taking up his spot and wrestling with his dad on cue. Then back into the coach he'd go until it was time for his next take. Not once did he falter – until, that is, on the last day of filming.

At the end of filming there is often a wrap party to celebrate. This film was to be no different, and I prepared food and drinks for the crew and actors who chatted as they prepared to sit around and relax for a bit on set. As Hercules was making his way back to the coach he glanced around and took note of what was happening and seemed to think to himself, 'Wait a minute. What's going on? It's a party!' There was no way he was being left out or going back into his quarters. He firmly plonked himself down among the crew and we had to ply him with shandy and titbits until he was ready to leave and climb back into the coach, certainly happy to be one of the boys.

Life at this point in time was happy and relaxed, and we travelled away to shows and public appearances and just enjoyed each other's company. Andy at that point was still wrestling men and he would be off down to England for the big venues. When that happened, I used to get a little nervous at the prospect of sleeping alone in the sprawling house. However, I had a remedy for the fear that I felt as the dark of night set in: I'd pop outside to Herc and the two of us would settle down for the night in the Hercmobile. I felt safe in the knowledge that I'd have a good night's sleep with him beside me and I was only ever disturbed by an occasional snore.

CHAPTER 15

MOVING ON

It was in 1987 that we came across a property for sale high up in the Ochil Hills in Perthshire. Sheriffmuir Inn had been on the same hills but further south. This new property had 30 acres of land, with a rundown old house and barns. It was ideal for all three of us. We could custom-build a property that would suit Herc, and I would be able to do more with my horses again.

The trip to the property was on a dreich – which is to say dull, drizzly – February morning, through Glendevon, with its magnificent hills shrouded in low cloud. I did wonder at that point in time how keen I really was to move, but Andy's never-ending enthusiasm pulled me back along with him and as we turned the last corner that led into the forest of the Dunning Glen, which branched off the main Glendevon

Road, I could see the potential. It was very private and it would be a great, safe place for Herc to live. Once again we were packing up and on the road to a new challenge. Big Bear Ranch was born.

The situation was stunning. It sat astride the top of the glen with magnificent views and wonderful scenery, but it was a challenge: practically everything would have to be knocked down and the old house, though it looked charming, was simply a damp and dreary, rundown old building.

That winter we submitted plans to Perth and Kinross Council. By now Hercules and his fame opened doors a lot more easily and the authority agreed that we could build a new house on the site of the old one and, more importantly, that we could keep Hercules in his new quarters. They, of course, as you can now probably guess, were to be built first and a beautiful new pool and gardens began to emerge beside the site for the house.

The following spring, it rained and rained. We had made a temporary home for Hercules in the old barns and he was happy enough to be near us and popped in and out with Andy to survey his new domain. We both lived in the coach as we prepared to start building.

First, we hired the builders, whose leader, 'wee Andy McLymont', f from Dunblane, we had known for many years. He was just over five foot of blue-eyed mischief. Andy was a skilled tradesman who liked to have fun and he constantly wound up the other two builders with his antics. He was in charge and his great skill helped turn things around quickly.

He'd chat away to Herc. 'Hi Hercky, how are you this

morning, my son?' he'd say cockily each day when he arrived. Hercules was quietly keeping an eagle eye on him and seemed to be ready for a little bit of fun every time he saw him. Herc always seemed to pick out characters, and eyed them with more mischief than was normal.

The builders set about their task, working hard through the cold muddy spring. As usual, Hercules's needs were to be met first, before ours were attended to, and soon his magnificent pool was ready. It took a week to fill it with clear springwater from the hills. The sun shone and the pool glistened. It looked fabulous, with its rolling lawns and fallen trees to lounge about in after a dip. The builders stood admiring their work, but, once again, wee Andy surprised everyone with his antics. He was keen to have a dip in the sparkling pool before it was officially handed over to Hercules. Without further ado, and to the amazement of us all, he stripped down to his underpants and, laughing to the accompanying wolf whistles, dived in. The initial shock of the cold water took his breath away for a moment but, being the tough wee cookie he was, he lifted his arm and roared, '*Braw!*' before gliding through the water. We all shivered at the thought, our teeth chattering.

What we hadn't noticed was that 'big' Andy had slipped away. He had quietly decided that, at long last Hercules would have some fun with this cheeky builder. Tiptoeing, cartoon-like, slowly out of his new den, Herc snuck across to the edge of the pool steps. He took one look in at the little man who had interested him so much over the last few months. His eyes lit up, and without any further hesitation he rapidly climbed in beside him.

Wee Andy had just started on a return swim towards the steps when he noticed that he had company. I never saw him move faster than he did then, as he quickly turned around in the water, panicking and uttering a good few expletives. We all stood and laughed, and Herc enjoyed the chase with a very cheeky look on his face.

Wee Andy just made the edge of the pool and clambered out, skinning his knees on the newly laid concrete, as Herc breathed down his neck, splashing his big paws in the glee of the chase. I'll never forget the sight of that wee man as his pants, heavy with water, tried to go south. But wee Andy had other, more pressing, things on his mind at that moment and made no attempt to cover his bare behind. For some reason, throughout the rest of the building project he never seemed inclined to attempt another swim.

Hercules was in seventh heaven, a happy, happy bear. After that day he splashed about in the pool at any given opportunity. His dad, Andy, would dive over his big head and try to outswim him to the other side while Herc tried to pull at his trunks or catch his trainers. It was sheer unadulterated joy, as was to be the majority of the rest of our days on the Ranch.

CHAPTER 16

'FIND HELP, MAGGIE!'

During our years at the Ranch we travelled away from home a lot to different venues and events, but we also did a lot of filming at home. The Ranch was an ideal location, set as it was in the midst of the softly undulating hills of Perthshire. At that time of our lives the phone rang constantly, practically every day, and it was always exciting when there was someone from, say, Germany, Japan, Italy or Australia on the other end of the line.

The Japanese, who had always shown an enormous interest in Hercules over the years, filmed everything when their crews arrived. You just knew that they would want to film every move you made. That was OK, though, because Hercules loved a film crew being around: he was never bored and didn't acquire the name 'one-take

Herc'for no reason! He was always ready to pose and have his picture taken.

In September 2000 we had a call from a producer at BBC Bristol. She sounded lovely and asked if we could travel down to Bristol with Hercules to film a production commissioned for a Disney educational programme about bears. It was to be a two-day shoot in the studios. It sounded great, and we accepted the job. We left it with her to make all the arrangements that we required for Hercules to be safe and happy.

It was a sunny late afternoon when we arrived in Bristol, all in a relaxed mood after a good journey, and we were quickly shown to an area at the side of the studios where we could park safely. It was soon time for tea and we were hungry after the long journey. I'd made up batches of Hercules's food before we left, and as he settled down to his meat-and-tomato soup with two veg, I pulled out our small dining table for Andy and me. By this time it was fairly late. The studio was deserted and quiet and we were eager to settle down for the night. The three of us were asleep in no time at all.

The next morning we woke fresh and ready to start the day. Herc was up and about for breakfast and he was eager to have a look outside. The producer arrived. She was terribly helpful in a kind and considerate way. She was there to help with anything we needed, she said, and was delighted to meet Herc and introduce him to the rest of the crew.

Inside the large studios they had built a really natural-looking habitat, suitable for a bear to roam about and look at the different rocks, plants and mosses. It looked great.

That morning I had noticed that Hercules was even more cuddly than normal. He had snuggled into my legs in the back of the coach and looked very contented. Later that morning, as we led him into the studio, he was immediately interested in his new surroundings. The film crew were all set up and ready to capture on film anything that Herc happened to do.

As usual, he just got on with it and ambled about very naturally, his big bottom swinging from side to side as he checked out the set, sniffing and overturning the stones and logs. Once again, though, I did notice that he wanted to snuggle up to me a lot as he waited for the crew to change their camera angles or the lights. I must say, I was enjoying all his affections as his big warm body leaned against my legs, and I stroked his head with his brown eyes gazing up at me.

That day's filming on set went like clockwork. The director was delighted; it would be 'more of the same tomorrow', he said. He was happy to be working with such a special bear that had no fear of people milling around him and close-ups were not a problem – Hercules was such an obliging professional.

After the days of filming, the three of us made our way back to the coach as everyone packed up and left. We followed the same routine as usual and all seemed quite normal. Herc dropped off to sleep quite quickly as Andy and I sat down to dinner, chatting happily about how successful the day had been.

Without warning, there was an enormous commotion

coming from Herc's quarters. We jumped up quickly and whipped back his curtains. What we saw then brought panic into our quiet night.

Herc was in pain, real pain. He was rolling about knocking himself from wall to wall, the pain seared across his big face. We were in shock as our adrenalin kicked in. We tried to calm and comfort him but nothing worked. Something was wrong and we seemed helpless in the midst of the trauma.

In that instant I thought he was having some sort of seizure or a heart attack. Herc's big eyes were wide with pain and fear. He couldn't understand what was happening. It was an awful time. Everyone but the security guard had gone home and so we were pretty much on our own in the sprawling studios. Andy and I were beside ourselves with fear and panic, feeling as if we were both losing the plot. We cried and bumped into each other, helpless as we tried to comfort our Big Son.

'You'll have to find help, Maggie!' Andy roared at me and I quickly took off and tried to find someone. Eventually, I managed to find the security guard and he phoned the producer of the show for me. She was shocked and said she would contact the vet, who was on standby, and all we could do was wait. It seemed to take for ever before they arrived, but in reality it was just about thirty minutes.

Steam caused by his massive exertions rose from Hercules and clouded the windows; he was hot and panting, his big tummy heaving. The worst of his pain seemed to have passed, but, to our horror, he appeared to be unable to move his hind legs. I felt sick and Andy was beside himself, fear etched across his face. The producer tried to reassure us as the vet stepped in to check Hercules over. It didn't take him long. 'It's obvious what's happened,' he said matter-of-factly. 'He's burst a disc in his back and it's severed the spinal cord. It's very common in big bears like him. You'll probably have to put him down.'

On hearing his diagnosis I thought I was going to collapse. My head spun as I tried to take it all in. After all he was the vet and seemed knowledgeable; we had worked with him before on a TV show at Border Television Studios Carlisle and had no reason to doubt him.

It felt as if our world had just collapsed. The vet left quickly. I was by now in floods of tears, upset by his cold diagnosis, but, surprisingly, Andy was just mad. Always in defence of his pride and joy, he raged. 'No *way* am I putting my big man down,' he vowed. 'I'll get him better, I'll get him better,' he ranted over and over, never one to give in to a situation until there was absolutely no alternative left.

CHAPTER 17

WORRYING TIMES

The producer had said goodnight. It was pitch black and once again it was just the three of us facing this enormous predicament together.

For the first time in his happy life Hercules seemed beaten, unable to understand as he lay on his tummy with his back legs splayed out behind him, my magnificent son now a sorry sight of helplessness.

We sat beside him for hours on the wood shavings in the back of the coach, stroking him and trying to comfort him as he looked to us – no mischief in his eyes now, only a bewildered stare. He seemed to be thinking, 'What's wrong with me?' And, as he was so used to our being there for him, he seemed shocked that this time we could do nothing for him. Eventually, he drifted into an exhausted sleep. We would have to wait until morning to find out what we could do.

When the producer and director arrived early that morning we had been ready to leave for a couple of hours. We had made our plans during the long dark night for what we were going to do.

First, we phoned our vet at home, John Tough from the Lanark veterinary practice. John was a handsome, ruddy-faced, kind and caring vet, always immaculate in his checked shirt and tie, with his tweed jackets and highly polished brown brogues. He wasn't one to give in easily, either. 'Right,' he said after we'd hurriedly told him what had happened, 'get up the road, get home as quick as you can, time is of the essence.' What he planned to do was to inject Hercules with a solution that was used on people who had serious spinal damage from car accidents and suchlike. The injection can greatly reduce the trauma to the spine if it is administered in a fairly short time from the incident. But he said Hercules would need much more than a single human being because of his sheer size. 'We'll have to try to find the solution from various hospitals so that there'll be enough,' said John. 'I'll get on to that and I'll be waiting for you at the Ranch with it when you get back.'

Finding enough of the solution was an enormous task. I phoned lots of our friends and they were dispatched on John's orders to various hospitals around the country, from as far north as Aberdeen to Carlisle in the south, all travelling quickly in the quest to be ready for Herc's returning home to Big Bear Ranch.

CHAPTER 18

UNCERTAIN FUTURE

We left the studios and set off on what was a quiet reflective journey home. John had at least given us some hope that all was not yet lost. We clung to that hope as Hercules lay in his quarters looking at us every now and again through the glass door with a puzzled expression on his face. In his innocent world he just couldn't understand how, in the blink of an eye, his normal life full of play and energy had dissolved into pain and immobility. Shock played across his face. Outside in the streets it was otherwise a normal sunny day with people going about their business as usual, unaware of the fact that we were in a daze, filled with a sense of that our lives would never be the same again.

That trip seemed to take for ever, both of us wrapped up in our own thoughts. Periodically, I'd pop in beside Herc and sit stroking his big furry cheeks as Andy drove. At last, we were home, exhausted but on familiar territory, the gravel of the courtyard crunching under us as the coach drew up at the front of the house. We both drew a sigh of relief. John was waiting, as he'd promised, and again hope lifted in our hearts. He had everything ready and, with words of comfort, he shook our hands and said, 'Right Andy, let's get on with this. The sooner Herc has this injected, the better his chances are of surviving whatever it is that's gone wrong.'

Without further ado, John was in the back of the coach, syringe in hand and ready to give us a fighting chance at least. Even though he had such a task to perform, he was still in awe of the handsome big bear on whom he was about to work. But Hercules never even moved. He just gave John a quiet look of resignation as if to say, 'It's OK – on you go.' John was quick in administering the drugs, separating Hercules's beautiful coat to find bare skin. Andy and I stood back behind him, watching the needle slide into our big guy, praying that the medication would help.

'That's it, Andy. All we can do now is let him rest and see if the drug will do its work. Nothing else for it.' We knew that John had hope, and it gave us a belief that things might turn out OK after all. But it was, we knew, a big ask.

After everyone had left, Herc was still sleepy, and so we decided that, as he would have to stay in the coach, we'd move him beside our bedroom window so we could keep an eye on him twenty-four hours a day in case he needed us during the night. Parked up, we gave Herc some sweet milky tea, which he eagerly slurped down, and left him to get some rest ourselves. We were completely worn out and settled back in the comfortable and familiar setting of our own home. It wasn't long till all three of us were asleep. Tomorrow would be another day, we still had a chance.

Dawn broke. Hercules had not stirred all night and we had slept the sleep of exhaustion. On our awakening, the reality of the past twenty-four hours came quickly to the forefront of our minds. We slipped some clothes on and, with a mix of dread and hope, went outside and quietly opened the coach door. Herc raised his head when he saw us, his demeanour quiet and accepting; he too knew things were far from good. He looked so pathetic lying there.

I gulped some air and blinked quickly, trying to stem my tears. Andy's deep sorrow was evident in his demeanour. His pride and joy was in a sorry state. He could hardly speak as he choked out the words, 'Hello, my Big Son. We're here. Don't worry, we'll get you better.' We both knelt beside him and stroked him in silence for a few minutes, lost in our own thoughts. Nothing seemed to have changed. His back legs were indeed paralysed. The enormity of his injury was totally apparent to us now in the light of day. Hercules didn't make any attempt to move. He just gazed up at us with ever-trusting eyes, looking to us, as usual, for reassurance.

John Tough, our trusty vet, visited Herc again that day. He was still very concerned as, obviously the drug would need time to work and he said that we would just have to wait and see what the outcome would be. After a cup of tea and a chat, he again left us with some hope and we again took the lifeline he gave us, eager to grasp any comfort offered.

CHAPTER 19

HOPEFUL SIGNS

That winter, as the temperatures dropped and the snow sprinkled the hills, the wind huffed and puffed its way towards Christmas. Hercules's coach was tight into the side of our house so that he would know we were there beside him. He cosied up as the slumber of partial hibernation took hold and was quite content to trust us with his life. He was still greatly restricted by the lack of movement in his back legs, but enjoyed his coffee and some of his tasty treats. Marks & Spencer's roast chicken and their fresh prawns were two of his favourites, so we were happy that he was having a good and varied diet to help in his recovery.

We had quickly fallen into a routine. Each and every day we faithfully massaged him gently. Andy rubbed his feet and turned him over. He loved the contact and seemed to be slowly growing a little stronger. He could now sit up on his bottom. Manoeuvring himself with his powerful shoulders, he'd watch us from his windows. This routine lasted for a full two and half months, with Hercules patiently leaving everything to his mum and dad. It was a long stay, but he was a bit perkier and not quite as totally helpless as he had been when his injury had first struck him down.

Andy now thought it was time to see if Herc had enough strength in his body for him to be transferred into his cosy log cabin. He started the coach and Herc's ears pricked up when he heard the engine turn. He had always been excited when he knew we were off on our travels together. This time, though, the journey was only a short one, across the courtyard a matter of a few metres, to get as close as possible to his den. I guided Andy as he shunted to and fro and quickly the Hercmobile was almost adjacent to the cabin. He jumped out and quickly opened the back door. Hercules pulled himself up into a sitting position and sniffed the cold winter air as he peered out, keen to see what was going on.

Amazingly, without any hesitation as the heavy metal steps clunked into place and the door opened, Herc seemed to know what we were trying to achieve. Slowly and rather clumsily, he shuffled his big bottom onto the top step. Using his power, he concentrated on the task of negotiating his way down to the ground. Andy and I looked on. The sight of him like that broke our hearts, but he stuck to his task and, after a few minutes, he managed to deposit himself on the ground with a bump. He knew exactly where he wanted to be: in his cabin. We gently encouraged him with our voices as he slid and slithered his way towards his familiar den, heaving himself dexterously with his giant forearms until he was back in place, cosy with the heat lamps above him. He swiftly settled down and heaved a sigh of relief.

The winter dragged on. Snow coated the ground, beautiful and challenging at the same time. Hercules slept and ate and we continued with our remedial work on him. The heat lamp cast an orange glow and we hoped that the rest of semi-hibernation would allow him to heal and gain more strength.

Spring at last started to peep around the corner with all of nature's fresh signs of rebirth apparent. Along with the spring came new enthusiasm: Andy had a plan. Hercules was a little stronger after his winter slumber and could now pull himself about, but still only using his forearms. We invited various vets and professors to come and see him, but they were not hopeful. The overriding factor seemed to be the initial advice and diagnosis given by the first vet who had attended him on that fateful night of the trauma in Bristol. They feared that there would be no improvement in his situation, with a gentle suggestion from one or two of them that he may have to be put down. This, though, was not in Andy's game plan. He was going to start the rehabilitation of his boy that spring with exercise in the pool.

And exercise it was. Eventually, Herc, spurred on possibly by the warmer days, obliged us, and tentatively slid himself into the sparkling water. At first his movements were supported by the pool edge but he quickly became more confident and his eyes lit up as the water gave him extra freedom to move.

For the next eight months or so – rain, hail or shine – Andy religiously walked the side of that pool back and forth, back and forth, hour after hour, day after day, encouraging Herc to move. One pair of trainers after the other was worn away, but Andy was spurred on by the love he felt for his big furry companion.

Slowly, very slowly, there seemed to be some strengthening in Hercules's hind legs. 'I'm getting him, Maggie,' Andy would say excitedly when he saw any progress. 'I'll get him back, don't worry.' His determination screamed out at you from his every pore. And so it went on. He was on a mission.

Then, one day, there was a definite sign of movement. Herc was standing and, helped by the buoyancy of the water, made his way tentatively across from one side of the pool to the other. Needless to say, Andy was ecstatic and I was amazed. It seemed such a long time since his injury that few in our position would have kept faith in the task confronting them. Andy's thorough determination to see things through had come to the fore once again.

From that point on, progress, though slow, was certainly evident, with the occasional hiccup of course. I could only wonder at the pair in front of me: if they had been training for the Olympics, I am sure they would have won a gold. Even I, who knew them both so well, felt a sense of wonderment at the bond they shared. Their training and strengthening sessions continued. Wobbly stances were taken.

And, eventually, Hercules started to walk!

CHAPTER 20

A SENSE OF DOOM

It was now the November of 1999, just over a year since Herc's injury had occurred. His faltering steps were slowly translating themselves into a proper walking movement. Everyone concerned was filled with a feeling of optimism for the future.

Christmas Day dawned and Herc walked slowly into the house. That year, he enjoyed his turkey as voraciously as normal, and he joined the family in the house once again for Christmas celebrations. But he was not quite the same bear. He was slower, certainly, and the injury had really taken its toll. His coat no longer had the same lustre, but we felt we were on the road to recovery.

The vets and professors were amazed, to say the least, but to Andy and me, more importantly, one thing was patently obvious: the first diagnosis had been incorrect, and it had almost robbed us of giving Herc another chance. The big fella's spinal cord was obviously still intact. If it hadn't been, all the work that had been put in would have been a fruitless exercise; the training would have come to nothing.

Once again, Andy had put his faith in his belief, in this case that he would get his Big Son walking, and that belief had carried them through. Now it seemed that the rest of the journey would be easier, simply a matter of letting nature and nurture do the rest. Good food, warmth and care were all on tap as we counted our blessings and thanked God that we had another chance to be together.

The darkening skies of January made for early nights, and nature was beckoning Hercules to sleep a little more. His natural instinct to keep safe kept him in his cabin, content to slumber and rise for coffee a little later in the day. We felt confident that spring would see him even stronger as we lavished all the time and effort we could muster on his wellbeing.

The chills of midwinter slowly dissipated, bringing clearer days and sweet signs of spring showing themselves once again. Obviously, the knowledge that we had now gained that Hercules's spine was still intact threw up endless scenarios. When he had been injured we had enquired about having him X-rayed to see what the damage really was, but we were told that it would be a fruitless exercise because there was not an X-ray machine that would see through the fat and muscle to his spine. We had reluctantly accepted that information at the time, but Andy and I were now insistent that, as the first diagnosis had been completely wrong, we would make our own decisions from now on.

So we contacted the Royal (Dick) School of Veterinary Studies at the University of Edinburgh and prepared to take Herc for his first X-ray. We were angry at ourselves for not having pushed for an X-ray in the first place and maybe, as they had said, it would not work. But we wanted to be sure that we were giving him every chance.

Herc had wintered well and we were hopeful that he would prosper as the weather took a kinder turn. He looked on from his cabin with great interest as we readied the Hercmobile for the road. It had been a year and a half since we had all travelled together, so it felt right as Andy backed the coach up to Herc's den, the familiarity of our old routine feeling very comfortable.

The steps were lifted into place at the back door and we crossed our fingers that Herc would manage to climb them into the back of his beloved bus. It wasn't easy for him as we tempted him with his favourite treats, but he slowly managed to clamber up and we saw the look of relief he seemed to feel at being back with us in his familiar routine once more. And what a relief it was for Andy and me too, as we set off for Edinburgh to meet Paddy Dixon, the renowned vet, who we knew would give him his very best efforts.

As usual, our every move was trailed and photographed by the TV crews and newspapers. They wished us well, as they had through the years of Hercules's traumas and adventures.

They had clearly gained a real fondness for our big fellow. The wheels of the coach skimmed their way across the Forth Road Bridge and soon we were at the veterinary college with plenty of time to spare. We parked, only to be surrounded as usual by inquisitive well-wishers and vet school staff and police. One by one they peered in to ooh and ah at the real live teddy bear we had on board.

Herc was in his element. Especially since his adventures in the Hebrides, he loved to have people around him. All the time, though, much as we appreciated everyone's kind wishes, at the back of our minds was the fact that his big body would soon be subjected to the anaesthetist's needle. This was not without risk in itself. We need not have worried, though: as Hercules lay in the building that housed the X-ray machine, the anaesthetist informed us that he had such a big strong heart that she could have kept him under for hours. She said she had never seen anything like it, as she fondly stroked her sleeping charge.

Paddy Dixon and his crew were all keen to get started on their task, and everyone was milling around their famous patient. Eventually, X-ray after X-ray showed, to our delight, that Hercules's spine was indeed intact, that there was no sign of damage to disc or cord, and, most surprisingly to the vets, the pictures were as clear as crystal. Andy and I felt justified in our quest to get Herc better, and that gave us even more hope for the future.

On arriving back home at the Ranch that day, with Herc still groggy from his exertions and the anaesthetic, we were full of chatter about the future, more sure than ever now that we had one: our big boy would be OK. The vets and we ourselves now believed that, although there was no evidence to be seen, Hercules had suffered from an abscess somewhere in his back and his pain had come from the pressure it had caused before it burst. The plan now was to administer strong, long-term antibiotics to counter the poison that might still be coursing through his body.

To help us with this we contacted Anne Logan, a good friend and a fantastic vet, who lived a bit nearer to us than John Tough, as Herc would now need her to visit him much more frequently. Anne was to be such a comfort to us in the following months with her soft voice and knowledgeable encouragement. She always arrived quickly when we needed her, no matter what day of the week it was. Her obvious love of animals helped us grow close as we toiled to get to the source of the infection.

To our horror, though, Herc seemed to take a turn for the worse. The progress he had made fell away, and, as autumn drew to a close, he went off his legs again, struggling to move about. We were devastated. An abscess can be a mighty fierce adversary tucked away hiding, the poison it produces traversing its way through an otherwise fit body. When dealing with an abscess you can only hope and pray that eventually the strong antibiotics would seek it out and destroy its poison – a waiting game with an uncertain outcome.

Eventually, after many visits and consultations with our vet Anne, we had a breakthrough. The poison from the abscess had tracked its way to the surface and found an outlet for its vile pus and poison just on Hercules's left hip. We hoped that this would aid us in its dispersal. Each morning and evening we washed the wound and flushed it out with hydrochloride and water to take away the debris. We hoped that, as the outlet had broken through and the drugs were still being administered, this would help us gain the upper hand against this persistent adversary.

It had been a long journey for all three of us. We battled away but, once again, fate took a hand. The cold weather dragged Herc back to a state of semi-hibernation. This time round, though, it wasn't a blessing. When bears hibernate their heart rate slows down drastically and so the passage of the antibiotics through Hercules's bloodstream slowed as well. We were really worried. We kept him as warm as we could, but nature's force was too strong. Herc became sleepier and I feared the worst.

Over the next two or three weeks Hercules seemed to be getting weaker. Andy could not accept that we would not win this battle, but I feared that this time the cards were stacked against us.

During that period I always found sleep at night but would invariably wake and lie with thoughts and memories filling my head until I had to rise in the midst of darkness and make my way out to my Big Son. I felt helpless as I lay down beside him and pressed my face into his thick coat, drowning in the sweet smell of his fur. Tears rolled down my cheeks silently as Herc would contentedly snuggle up to me in his innocent ignorance of how ill he was. There I'd stay until I'd make my way back into the house to sit and

cry unendingly till exhaustion took hold and I'd quietly
crawl back into bed with Andy, who was oblivious to my
nightly vigils.

CHAPTER 21

OUR
FINAL DAYS

On the morning of 4 February 2000 our first thoughts were as always of our big man. We dressed for the cold day and I made a pot of tea with lots of sugar and milk for Herc. Out we went to see him in his cabin, where he stirred from his sleep, cosy under the heat lamp, still interested to know what we were up to.

I stepped in to give him his sweet tea. His big tongue dipped slowly into the liquid and I gave him his morning hug. Andy chatted softly to him and I left them like that as I walked off to feed the horses. It took me almost twenty minutes to finish the horses' feeds and I left them champing happily, heads down. 'Right,' I thought, 'I'll get our breakfast now.' I made my way back down to the house. As I crossed the courtyard I saw Andy motionless, head down, leaning against the den. My heart raced as I crossed over to him. He turned to me, tears dripping off his chin.

'He's gone, Maggie. Your Big Son's gone.' His shoulders slumped as sheer dejection overwhelmed his mighty spirit. We stood shoulder to shoulder and cried as we looked down on the big fellow who had captured our hearts and filled our lives with joy. He lay still before us. His fight had gone, our charmed life was over.

We buried Hercules at home, helped as always by our dear friend and neighbour Davie Johnman and his yellow digger. He had helped us so much over the years, felt our pain and understood our love of Hercules. It was fitting that he helped us at the end of our journey. Herc lay in his gardens at Big Bear Ranch and we placed a bronze statue of a bear over his grave.

In 2013, to our delight, the community in North Uist who had been part of Hercules's Hebridean idyll so many years before, built a walk in his honour at Langass Woods, where they erected a life-size statue of him overlooking the island down to the sea. In 2015 we decided that we would like Hercules to be reburied near his statue. We were given permission to do so and now he lies at peace in Langass Woods, still visited by hordes of his adoring friends.

It's a fitting place for him. He was such an extraordinary bear who gave us so much more than we could ever have expected. He touched the hearts of millions. It's appropriate now that he lives on in the folklore of the Islands as he lies permanently sleeping in the woods. The myths and stories of his escapades will be for ever entwined.

In July 2015 we placed a memorial stone over Hercules's resting place. The inscription on t reads:

'Hercules the Bear lies sleeping here, watching over his beloved islands, resting in peace.'